Fire In My Bones

Jeff Mills

© Jeff Mills, 2017
All Rights Reserved

Cover by Clive Thompson
www.getclive.com

Dedication

This book is dedicated to my beautiful wife Christa who has been a tower of strength to me in times of difficulties and pain. I know my pain has been her pain. Christa is a person whom I have learned so much from, especially patience.

Endorsements

As an eyewitness of Jeff's first miraculous healing in Düsseldorf, and later as Missions Director of his sending agency, this book challenged me to increase my efforts in bringing the Good News of Jesus Christ to the lost.

The inspiring testimony of God's faithfulness and guidance, together with Jeff's typical good sense of humor, will certainly build up your faith and increase your desire to see God's glory be manifested here on earth.

Andreas Pestke, Director Globe Mission

Jeff Mills is an enthusiastic evangelist who inspires hope in the hopeless. He has led many people to genuine faith in Jesus Christ, and together with his wife, they have cared for the poor and needy with a love only God can give.

The secret behind their motivation to tirelessly invest in people others seem to care little for lies in their own personal experience of encountering Jesus who instilled a "fire in their bones" to share His life with all who will listen. I have walked with Jeff and Christa throughout their missionary career and can testify to their faith, love, and integrity while influencing many for eternity.

Brad Thurston, founder and former director of Globe Mission

I met Jeff in 1993 in the context of a Globe Mission training course in Germany. Until 2007 my family and I were also part of Globe Mission, which meant I could spend quality times with Jeff whenever the German headquarters invited their missionaries for a "Time of Refreshing" or our paths crossed on home visits. There was a connection between us right from the start and, despite seeing each other too little, we somehow managed to build a wonderful friendship founded in deep trust, honesty and transparency with each other, which, I believe, helped both sides going through some rough and difficult patches. Communicating via email has been intense at times and less intense at others, but we are still following each other's walk with the Lord even though God has led my family and I away from Globe Mission.

Perhaps this describes already what kind of guy Jeff is, or to be more precise, the kind of person the Lord transformed him into: honest, transparent, faithful, communicative, and willing to keep relationships going and growing, regardless of the circumstances. In reading his book you will pick up some other qualities which I have come to love and admire in him: his sense of humour, his zeal for truth, his relentless pursuit of God's calling on his life, his unwavering love for the Lord, his willingness to endure hardships for the greater good combined with his openness to live in dangerous places others wouldn't dare to go to, and his amazing integrity as well as humility. The most predominant trait, however, is Jeff's genuine love for Christ, and his longing to see as many people as possible experience the same intimate relationship with their Creator as he does.

In a condensed way, this book tells the remarkable story of a misfit and rebel being transformed by the love of Jesus Christ into a mighty warrior of God's Kingdom. It is worthwhile reading as it is both entertaining and very challenging, sharing that God's incredible, transforming and life-giving power is still at work and available to the lost. You might not be called to be a full-blooded evangelist like Jeff is. But regardless what and where your mission is as believer in the Kingdom of God, you can certainly get inspired to pursue your calling with the same zeal and dedication as Jeff does, to bring glory to God by bringing people closer to and into a firmer relationship with their Creator.

Gottfried Hetzer. Horsham/UK

Probably the first book I have read in one sitting! In typical no-nonsense style, Jeff's encouraging autobiography brings us key challenges for these days. Here is a man who audaciously presses through and dares take God at His Word.... so that 'God's will be done on earth, as it is in Heaven'.

Paul Cocking, Living Water Development Coordinator, Adopt-A-Child.com

I have known Jeff since the 90ies. I was a witness to Christ giving him the light of the gospel. He understood the grace of the cross of Jesus for his life, and the love of Christ burnt greatly in him and caused him to surrender and to live completely for Him. A very special gift was the fact that around the same time, his wife Christa understood the grace of Christ, and has lived together with him for the Great Commission of Christ as commanded in Mt 28:18 - 20. I had the great privilege to accompany Jeff and Christa in their first steps of faith, by baptizing them and to send them out as missionaries.

Jeff has become a model to me of zeal for the gospel, for the ministry to the poor as well as for generosity and perseverance. In spite of many a tribulation he has gone through, to my knowledge, he never thought of giving up and never once doubted God's goodness and wisdom.

I recommend this book to everyone who seeks to be inspired by a shiny example of the dedication to Christ's Great Commission: Go - to the end of the earth - preach the gospel and make disciples of Jesus of everyone whose heart God opens.

Carsten Buck, Pastor Evangeliumshaus Krefeld, Germany

I met Jeff Mills for the first time in 1995. He was a guest speaker at the yearly missions conference in our church. What struck me most right from the beginning was his zeal for the gospel, his genuine love for people as well as his burning passion for the lost. Ever since then, I have accompanied Jeff in my capacity as a missionary colleague and later as deputy director of Globe Mission. From what I have observed and witnessed, Jeff Mills is a man of highest integrity, who dedicates his life uncompromisingly to our Lord Jesus and the proclaiming of the gospel. He has proven this to the glory of God in numerous situations in his life and ministry in which he was cast down, but not destroyed. In all these years Jeff has become a dear and faithful friend to me whom I greatly respect.

His autobiography "Fire in my Bones" is proof for me that God can change any man who sincerely seeks Him. And it is the amazing and encouraging story of a man who walks with God and who God uses mightily to build His Kingdom not only in Guatemala but also India.

I hope it will inspire many readers!

Pastor Eduard Riepl, Ludwigsstadt, Germany

When we decided to come to Guatemala for the first time in July 2015 we were expecting to meet that ex-military British tough missionary. It didn't take few hours after meeting Jeff, to discover that he is funny, pleasant & easy to talk to. What impressed me the most is how he uses his physical illness and limitation in a funny & hilarious way. I never noticed that he is angry or upset at God for his health problems. This in itself has been a big witness to us.

In the meantime, he is a dedicated Christian who has spent so many years in a very poor country trying to offer spiritual and physical help to its people. I never heard him complain about being there nor did he express a desire to leave.

It was not easy to leave Guatemala, after our first visit, because of what we have seen in Jeff and his beautiful and dedicated wife, Christa.

I will never forget his many short visits to the clinic to give me encouragement and support while I was seeing patients. Not to mention the pleasure of having Christa, his wife, as my personal translator in the medical clinics.

Dr. Mark Michael MD., Ohio, USA.

Acknowledgments

I want to thank Val Waldeck for the many hours she has done proofreading this book, and also all the advice she has given me. Without her help, this book would never have been published. Thank you so much, Val. I am in debt to you.

Val is a Christian author and has written many books. She also runs an excellent course for people who want to become authors and have their books published. You can contact Val at www.valwaldeck.com.

Table of Contents

Dedication 2

Endorsements 3

Acknowledgments 7

Introduction 11

Chapter 1. The Early Years 15

Chapter 2. School Years 19

Chapter 3. My Military Days 23

Chapter 4. Christa – The Woman In My Life 30

Chapter 5. Life After the Army 35

Chapter 6. The Change 40

Chapter 7. The New Life 46

Chapter 8. My First Mission Trip 52

Chapter 9. Constanta and Miracles 56

Chapter 10. Back to Romania 59

Chapter 11. Unsettled 62

Chapter 12. My First Trip to Guatemala 65

Chapter 13. The Preparation 68

Chapter 14. Some of the History of Guatemala 72

Chapter 15. The Learning Period 75

Chapter 16. The Fun Begins 79

Chapter 17. The Change 85

Chapter 18. The Dangers 91

Chapter 19. The Ministry 94
Chapter 20. Health 98
Chapter 21. Feeling Sorry 103
Chapter 22. Preach the Truth 107
Chapter 23. India 110
Chapter 24. Second Mission to India 118
Chapter 25. Bad News 122
Chapter 26. The Untouchables 125
Chapter 27. The Way Ahead 128
Chapter 28. Are You Called to be a Missionary? 131
About the Author 135
Contact Us 136

Fire in My Bones   Jeff Mills

Introduction

My book is about what it is like to be a missionary. Life is not a bowl of cherries, but often the opposite. In spite of that, it is my hope is it will encourage others to join this special brand of peculiar people who have given all to reach the lost in another land.

It has taken me nearly ten years to complete this book, mainly because of being very involved on the mission field. Time has not been kind to me. However, I have made a concentrated effort to finish the book and get it out to print as soon as possible. It has been costly, and at times I have been misunderstood by others, but I have refused to allow them to get in the way of the dream God gave me many years ago.

My heart burns to share the Gospel of Jesus Christ with the lost. My heart also burns to see revival come to not only our town of San Miguel Dueñas, but the whole of Guatemala, as well as India where we have also ministered. I believe this will happen in my time here on earth.

I live for the revival that is unfolding and know it will surpass all previous moves of the Holy Spirit, bringing millions of souls into the Kingdom of God before the return of Jesus Christ.

Many have seen the video on the revival almost 27 years ago in the small town of Almalonga among the Mayan indigenous in Guatemala. It is still going on, the longest ever revival in the world. I have shared the Word in this town and the place blew me away. You could feel the Holy Spirit in the atmosphere wherever you went. I will be speaking about this later in my book. This is what I long for and might have begun to happen in one of our local churches, but sin got in the way.

The world today is experiencing a political and social upheaval. Governments are forcing changes on us unheard of twenty years ago. Sadly, the church is not weathering the storm any better. Strange teachings have crept in and many of us are like the proverbial frog in hot water, not only not noticing it but accepting these teachings.

The Word of God in Matthew 1:22 tells us in the end-times that even the elect could be deceived. If we want to see revival break out across the world, we need to stay daily in the Word so as not to be deceived. It does not mean throwing the baby out with the bathwater. We can cling to what is good as it says in 1Thessolonians 5:21. We have to forget the revivals of the past – as great as they were – and look to the greatest one that is coming. To see this happen, we need to tear down the walls that divide us within the faith.

I have visited many churches where there is no life. They are religious, controlled by the pastor who really does not understand anything about the Holy Spirit and then wonder why their members leave the church! A sheep goes where the grass grows better, and so does a Christian who is hungry and thirsty for more of the Holy Spirit. They are like me. They have fire in their bones for more of God.

Join me in my journey and see how God has kept my fire glowing throughout the years. This book is serious, but also at times humorous. You will hear about many of the trials and tribulations my wife, Christa, and I have been through and also some of the hilarious moments in our lives. I begin this story from my childhood to show you just how our wonderful Father in heaven will even pull the dreg of society into His loving arms.

May God touch you through it, speak with you, and perhaps even send you into the mission field, even though there is a great cost! There are still thousands of people throughout the world who still need Jesus

Christ as their Lord and Saviour. When the Lord says, "Whom shall I send?" (Isaiah 6:8), you can reply, "Send me Lord."

Fire in My Bones					Jeff Mills

Chapter 1

The Early Years

GO! Jesus' last command to all of us –

"Go therefore and make disciples of all the nations, baptizing them in the name of the Father and the Son and the Holy Spirit"
Matthew 28:19.

He didn't give this command just to evangelists or pastors. Jesus gave this command to every single born-again Christian. How many Christians can truly say they have fulfilled His last command to His people? There are churches fattening the minds of their members with more and more Bible teachings, courses, seminars, and concerts whilst failing to fulfill this last command? Is that your church? Only you can answer this question and then know what to do.

Jesus gave us the Holy Spirit to enable us to be bold and preach the Gospel whilst there is daytime. Many churches remain small for the very reason they do not share about eternal life. Ask yourself seriously, "How often do I share Jesus?" If it is not regularly, then you have a problem.

There is a Bible verse that challenges me, and everyone should remember:

"How terrible it will be for me if I do not preach the Gospel"
1 Corinthians 9:16b.

For more than ten years I have attempted to write this book about my time on the mission field, and always put it off with the excuse I was too busy as a missionary! But the Lord has now given me free time in-between the many surgical operations on my back. As you read, may the gentle voice of the Holy Spirit touch you. I am certain, once you have tasted life as a missionary, like my wife and I you will never want to return home!

My life before becoming a Christian was somewhat "colourful" to say the least. It's not necessary to share most the experiences I have been through in life. Suffice to say I was headed for hell, but my wonderful Father in heaven had other plans for me.

I will share some of my past, however, and how it led to my first becoming a born-again Christian, and then a missionary.

My father and mother had just arrived in England in 1947 after the fall of the British Empire in India, and I was born a couple of months later, the third of five children. It was not an easy time for my parents. I can still remember being sent out with my elder brother, Peter, and sister, Sandra, to pick wild raspberries so my mother could make pies.

My father, who fought in the Second World War in Burma, was a staunch Roman Catholic and Sundays meant a forty-five-minute walk to church, which I thoroughly enjoyed.

We used to pass over a small bridge. Someone had thrown an old water tank into the river and we would rush up to the bridge to see who would be the first one to throw a stone into the tank. I could not run fast in those days and was always last. Later in life I would win trophies for running.

The reason we rushed was to see how many stones we could get them into the tank in five minutes as that was all the time my father would give us. It was also fun to see my parents join in. Thinking back to this time, I am sure I was the champion stone thrower. I think we all enjoyed this more than church.

The minute we entered the church, we were told to be quiet. I could never understand why, so I asked my mother and she explained God was in the little box in front of the church. I often wondered how He managed to squeeze into such a small box and if He slept there all the time.

I tried to stay silent to avoid getting slapped across the head by my father, but that lasted about five minutes. I could never understand what the priest was saying. He always had his back to us and most of the church service was in Latin. I often wondered what country God came from where they spoke Latin.

I didn't bother too much with such questions. It was much more fun making paper airplanes from the weekly flysheets and throwing them across the church. That often resulted in a hard clip around the ear – and sometimes from the priest!

After the service, which went way above my head, the priest would stand at the back of the church saying farewell to everyone and giving them a handshake. Some Sundays he would look at me and just sigh! I could never understand why!

Through hard work, my parents moved to London and soon had their own bed-and-breakfast house, and later a hotel. They took good care of us.

In our younger days, my father insisted all of us had to have a spoonful of castor oil when we returned from church on Sundays. Somehow, I think he had the strange idea it kept us healthy! Even stranger, my father never once had a spoonful himself! One day the five-gallon jar of castor oil disappeared! I was the one who caused most problems in the house, so I got the blame! Years later I found out my elder sister, Sandra, had thrown it away, but she never told my father! He died still believing it was me.

I was always up to mischief. One day when nobody was in the house, I made a small fire on the living room carpet- I rather enjoyed it! But luckily, my mother returned from shopping. She could not get into the house because I had locked the door, so she knocked on the window, saw the fire, and nearly passed out with fright. The fire was getting bigger and the room filling with smoke.

I was terrified she was going to give me a hiding. I shouted to her, "Promise not to hit me and I will let you in."

"I promise, "she shouted, "but let me in immediately!"

I opened the main door and got her hand right across my face!

"You promised not to hit me," I retorted with great fear in my eyes.

By this time, she had put the fire out and there was a large hole in the blackened carpet. She took hold of my ear, sat on the sofa and lambasted my backside. I pretended to cry as she really could not hit hard, but a few hours later I was really crying when my father got hold of me!

Before we moved to London. we lived in a small village called Hookwood in Surrey. I had a good friend called Ian whose parents had a farm, and I spent hours with him helping to clean out the rabbit hutches. We were always rewarded afterwards with a cake or biscuit.

To get to his farm, I took a short-cut across a field that had cows and a bull in it. I was terrified of them, but somehow, I always outran the bull which insisted on chasing me. One day I fell flat into cow pat and went home smelling really bad.

I got so used to getting spankings I would often hide a book in my back pants. When my father or mother spanked me, I never really felt anything. But despite all the spankings, I knew my parents loved me as I always got a present on my birthday and at Christmas.

Chapter 2

School Years

My school years were not much to speak of. Most of the time I played hookey. No, not hockey, but hookey – another word meaning skipping school. I was a master at this! I think the teachers were happy when I was not there, so I never got reported when I was missing.

However, I did get swollen hands and backside from the leather strap laid into me for speaking in class, or making paper pellets and firing them at the girls' heads. It made me respect some of my teachers.

Today this type of discipline is forbidden and what a great shame it is, especially when we see that even murders are happening in schools across the world.

Fed up with my bad reports from the Roman Catholic school in Chelsea, London, my parents placed me in the very first secondary modern school in the UK – The Elliott School in Wimbledon, South London. There I enjoyed my studies, especially English history and music. which I excelled in.

But I was still up to mischief. One day I put ink into the fish tank in the laboratory classroom. I even threw one fish out of the window to see if it would fly! We had fun placing the trash bin over the gas taps, putting a flame to it, and seeing it fly into the air.

I made sure the biggest guy in the class became my friend. When other boys wanted to fight me, I hid behind my friend, Brian, who would soon sort them out for me. We often went into the cellars to smoke a cigarette. The boiler-man allowed us into his "office" and there we were safe to smoke.

There was a very old cemetery next to our school and one day some gang members tried to put me in an open grave. Luckily, Brian came along at the right moment and they all ran away. That is what I call wisdom… having such a friend as Brian. Sadly, I heard in his later years he turned to crime and I lost contact with him- I am glad I did, as often we "borrowed" a motor scooter and went for joy rides. How we never got caught by the police I will never know.

There were many pupils at The Elliott Secondary Modern School who later became famous. It is hard to believe I am actually included in the famous pupils' website! You don't believe me? Look at the website http://www.elliottonians.com/reference/notables/notable-pupils.html.

I am right next to Pierce Brosnan, the James Bond actor. I think I look pretty smart stuck in-between these people! Some of the members were in famous pop groups back in the sixties.

Weekends we loved to go swimming at the local swimming baths. This is where all my family learned to swim, including me at the very young age of four years. I loved swimming and was soon entering the school swimming competitions and winning trophies. I was not a strong-muscled boy, quite the opposite really! I was scrawny, but boy could I swim fast! I also loved athletics. The triple-jump and running the mile were my favorite sports. This was a race I never won, but always came in the first three.

After my school years, I got a job working in a local factory. The pay was not much, but to me it was a fortune. This was-my first-ever real money, even though I had worked for a few years as a paperboy delivering the daily papers. It was fun meeting all the men and women at work. The men always laughed at me as I was the youngest man in the firm. I really didn't care and it was there I met my first ever girlfriend. I can't even remember her name, but I know my heart was going faster than a puffer train. We went to the local cinema, sat in the back, and kissed most of the time. I soon got fed up with her and she was making my lips sore, so I ended that relationship.

My weekends were spent with my friends drinking at the local pubs and dancing at the local dance hall. In those days, you had to wear a jacket and tie to get into the dance hall. The hall was never dark like the discos are nowadays and at least you could see who you were dancing with. I fell in love with the girl who sang each week, but sadly she did not fall in love with me!

In the local pubs, my friend always wanted me to play my harmonica with the band that was playing. It took a couple of pints of beer, which they bought for me, to build up enough courage to play. I thoroughly enjoyed that, except when I had one beer too many and got out of tune with the band! It was an instrument that came naturally to me at the age of six.

My friends and I took turns to drive a beaten-up old van each time we went out so someone was always sober enough to drive us all home. Unfortunately, one night my friend forgot he was driving. He had a good amount of alcohol in his system and decided to drive over a roundabout instead of around it. We hit a truck and then a car, spun like a top, and landed upside down. It was truly a bad accident and we could all have died.

We were knocked unconscious. My head was stuck between the roof and the floor. The three nurses we were giving lifts to could not do too much as they, like us, were – unconscious! I do not remember the firemen cutting through the car to get me out. I was going in and out of consciousness but I do remember hearing some voices saying, "He can't possibly be alive after this bad wreck." I also remember thinking to myself, "No way am I going to die."

In the ambulance on the way to hospital I remember looking down on my body as the ambulance personnel pumped away at my heart. This was the first time I had a spiritual experience, and I could see one of my friends with his arm and head all bandaged up looking at me anxiously. I was peaceful, but then I woke up in the local hospital with my worried mother looking at me! I couldn't speak as I had broken my jaw, fractured my skull, broken a few ribs, and an arm, but all I complained about was that my little finger was hurting me! There was glass everywhere in my body. I was screaming out in pain, and that was hard with a broken jaw.

The next seven weeks were so painful and murderous. My teeth were wired up and I was not able to eat anything solid. Had I been fat it would have been a good way of losing weight, but I was already skinny! However, I was pleased I could continue to drink beer. The only problem was my stomach had shrunk through lack of solid food, and I could only manage a pint before feeling tipsy! The hospital was so concerned they gave me a set of pliers should I ever think of throwing up.

The next few weeks were spent looking at juicy steaks in butchers' shops and I even attempted to shove some strawberries between my teeth! I could not watch my family eating their meals and always went out at meal times. Later, my mother warmed up clear soup which I drank through a straw. I really felt sorry for myself in those days!

To make matters worse, the local pub I always went to was informed not to allow me more than one pint of beer! But I did manage another two or three which my friends bought for me. Let me tell you, I would rather break any other bone in my body than my jaw.

Years later I would regret saying that!

Chapter 3

My Military Days

BY THIS TIME, my parents had almost given up on what to do with me. My father suggested I join the British Army and learn a trade, but his only worry was I would end up in the military prison.

I wanted to join the police force and go into detective work, but they talked me out of it. I am so glad they did or I would never have met up with my beautiful wife-to-be. I decided it was time to prove my father wrong, and so in 1965 at the age of seventeen, this scrawny figure arrived in the REME Recruiting Depot in Arborfield, Berkshire, to begin a career that would last 23 years and reach the dizzy heights of Warrant Officer. Now my father was proud of me!

The basic training was murder! I shared a room with twenty other men. Every morning a screaming lance corporal woke us up at 5.30 am. First we had to run a mile, then come back, shower, and go for breakfast.

After breakfast, we dressed in our best uniform for inspection. Proudly we marched onto the square, our leather boots shining like mirrors from hours of spit and polish, After the inspection, it was back to our rooms, a quick change into battledress and then another mile run around the square carrying our 7.62 rifles above our heads. It was agonizing and if we so much as dared to lower the rifles, we were forced to run around the square again.

Some people dropped out and paid their way out of the army, but I refused to give in. I wanted my father to say to me, "I am proud of you son." Sadly, that never happened. He never came to my Pass-Out day. All the other soldiers had their parents there, but only my sister and mother came. That hurt me a lot.

My first posting in the Forces was to Bergen, Belsen, in North Germany. The infamous Bergen Belsen concentration camp, where thousands upon thousands of Jews were murdered in the Second World War, was just down the road from the regiment. I often went there and looked around the massive graves where up to ten thousand Jews were buried. I was a practicing Roman Catholic in those days and prayed for their souls and families.

Being there left me with a strange feeling. It was eerily quiet and I did not see one bird fly over the area. It was an horrific time. The camp was designed to hold ten thousand prisoners, but in fact held sixty thousand. The famous Anne Frank and her sister died in this camp. I remember taking a black and white photograph of her grave. I wept as I thought about the sadistic medical experiments carried out on many prisoners. This will always be in my memory. One needs to see one of these horrific concentration camps just to understand how evil man can be.

In Hohne, Bergen, I was attached to a very famous British Regiment called the 11th Hussars (Prince Albert's Own). It had a history of fighting in the famous Battle of Balaclava – "The Charge of the Light Brigade" in 1854. The regiment also fought at the Second Battle of El Alamein in October 1942. It took part in the Allied invasion of Italy in September 1943 and after the Normandy landings in June 1944, took part in the North-West Europe Campaign. They also fought in the desert with the Seventh Armoured Brigade (The Desert Rats).

Its new uniform by coincidence included "cherry" (i.e. crimson) coloured trousers, unique among British regiments and worn since in most orders of uniform, except battledress and fatigues. I actually blew the bugle used in the Charge of the Light Brigade, of which a film was made.

Little did I realize at the time that soon we will be hearing a trumpet being blown for the return of the King of kings, O hallelujah!

> *"Then the seventh angel blew his trumpet, and there were loud voices shouting in heaven: 'The world has now become the Kingdom of our Lord and of his Christ, and he will reign forever and ever'"*
> Revelation 11:15..

I stayed there for two wonderful years. I was not actually a member of the regiment, but attached to it. I belonged to the REME (Royal Electrical Mechanical Engineers), and our small group were in charge of repairing the Chieftain tanks. It is quite something to be on maneuvers and see these tanks in action. I went on many maneuvers during my time with this regiment. We were always prepared in case war broke out somewhere.

Later, I was promoted to Lance-Corporal before moving on to Bahrain in the Middle East. During this time the British were fighting the Arabs in Aden. I was back in the Headquarters, but very involved in what was going on there.

It was relatively safe where we were, except for some attacks from terrorists, so we swam, played soccer in 50 degrees centigrade (122 Fahrenheit) heat which gave us an excuse to drink beer in the evenings. I remember coming back from Bahrain so black from the sun, I had to show the customs officer I was really British by removing my watch so he could see the pink skin. Later he told me he was only joking with me. I was concerned in case he wanted me to drop my pants!

I kept myself super fit while in the army by playing every sport that was available. I was a sport freak! Soccer and Squash were my favorite sports, although I swam in competitive games as well as playing hockey. My hobby was winning cups and medals, which I excelled in. I think my father would have preferred me to stick to hockey like my elder brother, Peter, who represented Great Britain in two Olympics. I excelled in hockey, but soccer won the day!

I am sure my father did not like the other sport I excelled in – playing poker! In the evenings until late into the night, I won heavily, which led to many accusations of cheating, and that, in turn, led to fights!

In an attempt to show my father I was not that bad, I always went to mass in the local military Roman Catholic Church on Sundays! I think you could call me a Doctor Jekyll and Mister Hyde, leading two kinds of lives… or maybe a hypocrite!

During my time in Bahrain. I did not have a girlfriend but had a number of pen-friends, which kept me busy and out of mischief. The only problem I had at work was with my boss. He was a Captain and had a refrigerator in his office stacked full of Tiger beer. Saturday mornings were dedicated to emptying that refrigerator of beer! He was very generous and I generally staggered back to my room.

A year later I was promoted to Corporal. I returned to England and met one of my pen-friends. She was to become my wife and mother to our wonderful three boys, Philip, Dean, and Jon.

If anything calmed me down it was these great boys. They were the love of my life and I did not want them to become what I had been. I taught them all the worldly morals they should walk in, even telling stories and praying together at night time. Being a Roman Catholic, I had an altar in their bedroom with Jesus, Mary, and Joseph. I really enjoyed this time of praying with them and telling them stories they will always remember, like The Magic Faraway Tree."

I am very proud of my three sons. Philip matured very quickly and grew up to be a very strong man. He took up hairdressing and won a Southern England Best Women's hairdresser award. (Now you ladies need to book well in advance!)

Dean went into electronics and could often be seen repairing electronic cash registers across England. Jon is an author and has published a number of thrillers on Amazon.com. We keep in contact through emails and phone calls and I love to hear from them.

Whilst in the Forces, we moved regularly between Germany and England. And the wife and I got used to packing all our belonging into boxes. I know she did not like it, but I had signed up for the full twenty-three years. I had to participate in many military exercises which kept me away from my family, and sadly this led to a divorce which ripped my life apart. I could not believe my wife had become involved with other men.

It is a known fact that the highest divorce rate in Great Britain is among members of the Forces. The pain was just too much for me and I often wept. My only consolation was drinking beer. Over the years, I forgave her, but the hardest part was the separation from the boys.

I started to hit alcohol hard, moving on to hard liquor, but continued in the Roman Catholic Church. I felt so empty inside as I cried out to God. How could He allow this to happen to me? It seemed He never answered me... or at least, I did not hear him. I was desperately seeking God, but He seemed so far away. Little did I know Jesus said:

"I will never leave you or forsake you" Hebrews 13:5.

At this time, my dream was to get a posting to Hong Kong, but I received one to Cyprus. Sadly, I had to cancel this posting and go back to England so I would be able to see my children at least during weekends. I was posted to Wembley, London, to a top-secret establishment which cannot be mentioned here for security reasons. Here I was trained in "Interviewing Techniques." I did not like the job much, even though I did not have to wear my uniform most of the time. They made me sign an "official secrets" form which stopped me talking about my work for twenty-five years. Well I am past that now, but still feel better not talking about it.

Later I was posted to Andover in Hampshire, another place I would rather not talk about. To this day I still have not told my wife about my work there. Andover has such a beautiful countryside with many small villages and homes with thatched roofs. Here I became a good friend of Dave Kenton-Barnes. He is the only man I have seen roll up a home-made cigarette with one hand.

Dave often went to the horse races, which were not far from where we were. He was an expert at picking losers! We often had heated discussions about abortion. As a Roman Catholic, I could not believe millions of women across the world murdered their babies, mainly for cosmetic reasons. Sadly, my friend Dave committed suicide. That was a real blow for me.

I met a lovely girl here and we stayed friends for nearly two years. She helped keep me sane and from becoming an alcoholic. But I was still feeling empty, and though I was seeking God, He seemed so far from me.

Eventually I was posted to the Depot REME in Arborfield, Hampshire, where I first joined up. Now I was a Warrant Officer and no longer frightened of the Regimental Sergeant Major who screamed at recruits that they were not allowed to walk across the parade ground. Only God was because he couldn't see Him!

We became good friends and I started to enjoy life again. Soon I was made church warden in our military camp Roman Catholic Church. I loved keeping the building clean and preparing it for the Mass service on Sundays. The military Priest also held a service each morning at 6.30 am. Most times only he and I attended. I was an alter server and often enjoyed going into the building in the evenings and playing the church organ, but God still seemed far away.

I had a Bible and took it everywhere with me, but I noticed few Roman Catholics ever brought one to church. The Bible made no sense to me as I read it.

One Sunday the Priest asked where the two bottles of wine were for the Mass. Sheepishly, I said I didn't have a clue and it was a miracle they had disappeared! I think I was his best customer in the confessional box.

One evening we had a fancy-dress event and I decided to wear the Roman Catholic Priest's Mass clothes. My friend was dressed as a Monk and that afternoon we went out in my car to visit some pubs. Wherever we went, we were offered free drinks. Eventually we were stopped by the police. My friend was throwing up at the time and they asked me what was the matter with him.

I was shaking and afraid we were about to get locked up for drinking and driving, I lied and said, "My friend is a Monk and belongs to a closed community. They allow him out once a year, when he is allowed to speak. I am looking after him."

The policeman looked at me in concern and asked whether he needed to go to a hospital. I wanted to burst out laughing. "Thank you, Officer. I said, "but I will get him home now. He just needs to rest."

As the police drove off, I looked up at my friend who was now doing a dance and bundled him into the car. We returned to the barracks just in time for the party!

I am truly ashamed now when I think back to the crazy things I have done and got away with it. I do not recommend anyone should even attempt to do what I did

Chapter 4

Christa – The Woman In My Life

I was posted to the Ministry of Defense in London in 1980 where I undertook "interviewing" recruits. Again, I was allowed to wear civilian clothes and also to grow my hair long. "You mustn't look too much like a soldier," I was told.

My work was top-secret, and all I can say is it was very interesting! After two years of "training" was complete, I was moved to a military unit in Wetter Ruhr, Germany. There were more Germans than soldiers – something I liked as it meant no silly military exercises. I thought I deserved this peaceful place where German civilians repaired military tanks and other vehicles for use in the two Iraq wars and elsewhere.

My peace did not last long. One day the place was invaded by my friends from the Secret Service. The Commanding Officer, who was a Brigadier, was placed under house arrest and files were taken away from our offices. Many of us were interviewed and then began the game of "who squealed on the Brigadier?" The following day he became front-page news of a national tabloid newspaper in the UK, accused of misuse of funds, slush funds, etc. Suddenly we all became very famous! The Brigadier was quietly "retired" and life continued to its normal slow pace.

On my first day at work, I parked my car, and brushed down my uniform, which I had pressed until you could press no more. I looked up to see many people staring at me through different office windows. One of those women was the person who was destined to help turn my life around.

I knew I was looking very smart in my uniform and I was truly proud to wear it. However, all those faces looking down at me made me somewhat nervous.

In this new military unit we had many dinner and dance nights, where we dressed in our best dinner suits, blue and gold-laided with our medals. It was here I was to meet someone who would change my life forever! No, at this stage it was not Jesus, but a very beautiful German girl called Christa-Maria Posner.

I had only been in this establishment three days when this lovely young woman knocked on my office door.

"Come In!" I said sternly, busy looking down at my work. Then I looked up and saw this lovely German woman. She introduced herself and said, "Danke schoen fuer die Einladung!" In English she had said, "Thank you for your invitation!"

There was to be a formal lady's dinner-night that weekend. I had said I would not go as I was the "new man on the block." But a friend of mine had gone to see Christa (without my permission) and said I had invited her to the dinner-night!

"Oh, right! Hmm, yes, see you there!" I spoke half-choking!

Off she went, happy as a baby who had just had its nappy changed! I laid my head on the table, sighed, and thought to myself, "Oh no, here we go again!"

The afternoon of the event, I ironed my dinner suit and polished my shoes to the point you could see to comb your hair. I was a little bit worried, but thought to myself it was only a dinner night and I was not interested in having a girlfriend again. But that night it was love at first sight! We both fell in love as we danced until the early hours of the morning. I didn't want the night to end, but it finally did at 4am!

Now I was spending most of my time away from the bar and with Christa! Suddenly my life was worth living again. Here was someone who sparkled so much I knew she was worth more than any expensive jewel in the world. She was like a light shining in the darkness.

In the months ahead, however, Christa noticed I was always at the Roman Catholic Church every Sunday and then often at the "church bar." I think I was called a hypocrite in those days, but am not certain.

Christa had "signed off" from the Roman Catholic Church; something one must do in Germany if your belief in Roman Catholicism comes to an end because it is compulsory for every Roman Catholic in Germany to pay church tax. I am sure that keeps the Pope in Rome very comfortable.

I often think of the Bible verse:

"Even foxes have dens to live in, and birds have nests, but the Son of man has no place even to lay his head" Matthew 8:20.

Are we truly called to live in palaces, like kings, whilst serving God?

When you sign off from the Roman Catholic church, you cannot participate in their services or get married in their churches, let alone be buried!

The word "religion" comes from the Greek word "bound" and now I know why! It was not long before I too left the Roman Catholic Church after doing a long and thought-provoking study on them; I concluded it to be a false religion! To think I had worshipped Mary and other saints made me shudder. I also noticed how the Roman Catholic Church had changed the Ten Commandments. If you do not believe me, just look at a Roman Catholic Bible and compare it to a Protestant King James Version of the Bible. "Thou shalt have no other gods before Me" (Exodus 20:3) is the clear teaching of Scripture. Let me tell you, dear reader, there is only one King and one God whom we worship, and that is King Jesus!

I met Christa's parents. They were lovely people, but my German was not too good, so Christa was forever translating. I soon picked up the language and now speak it almost fluently. Christa's father, Otto, was a hunter and we often ate wild boar or deer. I loved being invited to eat at their house. Her mother, Elsa, was a great cook. They were both Roman Catholics and were somewhat concerned we had both left the Church.

Christa and I were happy going places together hand-in-hand. My life was certainly changing, but somehow I felt something was still missing, even though I had a wonderful girlfriend. We attended many dinner-nights and even met Prince Philip when he visited the military unit. This was the second time I had met him.

I continued keeping fit by playing squash nearly every day. Every year each soldier had to do a "ten-mile bash" fully kitted up and in a certain time limit´. I excelled at it. Some failed and I loved doing the last mile running backwards just to show off.

As fit as I was, I was still breaking bones playing soccer and squash. Christa eventually decided it would be a good idea to take up table tennis (ping pong). If you know the game, you will know the table comes in two halves. One evening I was playing when the table closed on my wrist. Another broken wrist for the second time! The numbers of broken bones was adding up! I considered taking up chess, but then decided it was not a good idea as I would probably punch the other player if he won!

So I took up going to watch Borussia Dortmund football as their ground was close by. To this day I still watch Borussia Dortmund, but only on television Saturday mornings. I call it Breakfast with Dortmund. I remember one day watching a match at the ground with some friends. There was no score, so two minutes before the end I started to leave. One minute before the end Dortmund scored a goal. I raised my hands with joy… not realizing I was now in the middle of the opposing team's fans. They started kicking and chasing me as I ran out of the grounds and straight into a policeman who wanted to arrest me until I told him I was the innocent party.

Chapter 5

Life After the Army

Soon Christa and I got married and life was good. We went on holidays to Greece twice a year, a country with so much history that we loved so much. I especially like Patmos, the island where John wrote Revelation in the Bible. I could imagine him sitting at the entrance to a cave and looking out across the beautiful blue and green colors of the Mediterranean. It was so peaceful.

Christa and I went back again and again. But travelling on a boat from island to island did not go well with my stomach and I would often be seen hanging over the edge of the boat feeding the fish! On one such occasion a local fisherman decided to help me by throwing a bucket of sea water over me when I was least expecting. Well, it worked! I was too shocked to be sea-sick at that moment!

We really enjoyed buying bread and cheese and sitting outside the local café's drinking coffee. But something was missing in both of us both and we did not know what it was.

A year before I left the military, my back troubles started. I played many rough sports whilst in the Forces and this had not helped my back to be very stable. I even played rugby once, but then decided the guys were too big for me. I had been flown back twice to England from Germany to a military hospital in London to have operations on my lower spine. Neither of the operations really helped much. I left the

Army after twenty-three years' service with a forty-five percent disablement pension and in a lot of pain.

Now that I was living in Germany, I started looking for a job. Unfortunately, there were certain ranking officers who really did not want me to have a civilian job with my last army unit. They did everything to stop me. I believe their reasoning was they were not able to discipline me because of my work. Even though I was not a Christian, I had certain moral standards which did not sit right with the hierarchy! For example, I would not lie for them and that stopped me getting a commission upwards to the next rank.

Luckily, I had friends in high places who got me in through the "back door" in a job as a helper. It was a start! Being a warrant officer in charge of 200 people, now sweeping the floors was a bit embarrassing for me. It was far more embarrassing for the officers, however, who had to face the German people's questions as to why they allowed one of their own officers get such a lowly job.

They were more offended than I was and I just loved seeing them trying to avoid making eye contact with me. I did my best each day to walk past them and say, "Good morning!" I loved watching the look on their embarrassed red faces! They tried everything to get me dismissed, but I had also joined the German Union – the first ever British man to do so!

By this time, the officers believed I was working as an under-cover agent for the higher echelons in the Ministry of Defense. The civilian unions also thought I was a spy for the military. This was real James Bond stuff, especially as Pierce Brosnan (James Bond) went to the same school as me! Sometimes I think they should have made me the James Bond!

My actual job as a civilian was a blessing in disguise. Soon I was to get a slightly better job checking the various spare parts for the military tanks each day. That only took me half an hour, and so I had plenty of spare time. I was totally unaware God got me into this job so I could use the time to learn more about Him!

One day as I was fooling around with some of the German workers, my back suddenly seized up. I could not move and the pain was unbearable. The Germans knew I fooled around a lot and they weren't sure whether to laugh or be shocked.

"Get on with your work Jeff!" shouted my supervisor.

"I can't, I'm stuck, and the pain is unbearable!"

He saw my face turning pale gray. Shock was setting in and he realized this time it was the real thing. Soon the sound of sirens filled the air as the ambulance drove right into the workshop.

Dracula's screams could not have been louder than mine as they unceremoniously laid me on a hospital stretcher.

I heard the guys joking. "Don't forget to clock off, Jeff!"

"Give me your Borussia Dortmund football club season ticket if you die, Jeff!"

I did not find that at all funny at the time.

Why do doctors always prod the injured place and ask if it hurts?

Three doctors later agreed I had a spinal injury. "We want to do a lumber puncture, Herr Mills," they said, trying not to smile.

I had one of these before and knew they were not very nice. "Well I am not going anywhere, Doctor, so do what you need to do, but I'll sue you if I die, "was my agonized response.

After a tomography, they came with that large needle. If I could have run right then, I think I would have beaten the world record for the 100 meters' race. As that seemingly ten-foot needle went into my back, I screamed and then passed out, totally unconscious into a nice, quiet world. If I ever needed God, it would have been at that very moment of time, but at this stage I seemed worlds away from Him.

Weeks later, after being discharged from hospital I was re-admitted as the pain in my back had worsened. They sent me to a specialist hospital where I was placed in a room with three other men.

Have you ever tried to sleep in a room where there were three level decibels of snoring? Certainly, the Bible verse in Jeremiah 31 did not seem to apply to me that night.

> *"At this I awoke and looked around. My sleep had been pleasant to me" Jeremiah 31:26.*

In the morning, I was weary after not being able to sleep. A gathering of doctors (or are they called a pack of doctors?) in white coats came by my bed. The smallest man seemed to be the big boss. He listened intently as one of the other doctors said in a medical language I did not understand, "This patient has a back problem…"

He grabbed my leg and twisted it so violently, I screamed in a voice that only a tenor singer could reach. Was I angry! I told this professor in front of his gaggle of students, "If you ever do that again, I will screw your neck the same way! and, that I am not just a patient, but have a name – Herr Mills."

I could see the student doctors smirking and the professor's face turning bright red as he moved on quickly to his next "patient."

Later that day a doctor told me the professor I had so rudely spoken to was the top surgeon in Germany.

"I really do not care who he is, and he certainly will not touch my body again!" I replied,

I knew it was time to escape. I did not want to be operated on by someone who just might not like me. I had visions of coming out of that hospital minus my spine, so I transferred myself back to the first hospital I was in. Months later as the pain continued to get really bad I was eventually operated on for the third time and had a disc removed. The recovery time seemed like years. In fact, it was years!

Able to work again despite the pain, I was placed in a job where I hardly had anything to do. But then the pain became so bad, I could hardly walk. I was put on sick leave, and eventually fitted with a tube directly into my back so I could pump pure morphine into it.

I started to drink alcohol heavily. It helped take some of the pain away. Some days Christa found me on all fours in tears. It seemed to be the most comfortable position to be in. For four long years, Christa helped me to dress and shower. She put me in bed and got me out of bed as I got worse. I thank my wonderful wife for all she did for me during this dark period of my life. It is wonderful to me that God has taken all those memories away from Christa.

Chapter 6

The Change

While I had been working as a civilian for the British Army in Germany, an Englishman by the name of Paul Baker came to see me just about every day. I knew what was coming! He was one of those born-again Christians who seemed so happy, almost as though he had just won the national lottery. At that time, I didn't know it, but he actually had something even better than any lottery, and that was Jesus Christ. I couldn't run very far because of my back injury, so when Paul came over, I had no choice but to listen to him.

"Jeff, do you know Jesus Christ as your Savior?" That was the first question I remember him asking me.

"Paul, I am a good Catholic. I go to church most Sundays, I have never harmed anyone, and I pray to Mary," was my reply.

"Jeff, I asked if you knew Jesus Christ, not if you knew of Him," responded Paul.

I was not in the mood to argue. The pain was returning and I needed a shot of morphine. I asked him "politely" to go away or else I would thump him.

Where was God when I got injured? Where was God when I was searching for the answer to why I was even born? Where was God in all this pain? Why would He allow me to suffer so? Was He real?

I still believed in God, but He was far, far away. I even attempted suicide on two occasions, but failed miserably when the rope broke! I was really angry with God and everyone else. I remember my mother saying she became pregnant with me at the wrong time because the British had to leave India after it became independent from Great Britain. I felt terrible rejection and really just wanted to die. I remembered how I had joined the army to die, and yet was never sent to the front line. Again, looking back, I knew God had other plans for me.

There was a time in my life when I nearly became a Jehovah's Witness. They never stopped bothering me after I spoke to one of them. The Germans have a law that people are not allowed to approach you first with their material. But once you have made the approach, they never leave you alone. They were like a magnet!

I was curious through and read much of their material, hoping it would bring me closer to finding the truth – Jesus Christ. However, I could not bring myself to accept some of their beliefs. Jehovah's Witnesses do not believe in the Trinity; they do not believe Jesus is the Son of God; and they have been proven time and time again to be false prophets. The Bible tells us to beware of false prophets.

"And many false prophets will appear and will deceive many people" Matthew 24:24.

My pain continued to worsen. Many times I just felt like packing it all in and calling it a day. Maybe an overdose of morphine would bring me peace. I thought. But God was not going to allow that to happen to me. Once more, I again thought of suicide, but I decided not to do it in case it hurt me. Not only that, I still had half a packet of cigarettes!

My friend Paul continued to harass me daily. Always talking about Jesus. He invited me on a number of occasions to come to a home group of Christians. He knew I could not run away because of my injury.

Over the new few months, no amount of threatening would make him go away.

"Jesus loves you so much, Jeff, and He doesn't want to see you go to hell."

Now that made my ears prick up! "Hell? Hell? I can't go there, I am a Catholic. Anyway, I will go to Purgatory… at least that is what the priests told me." I thought to myself.

I had heard Purgatory was a hotel in the sky somewhere. You didn't have to pay to stay there. The length of your stay was decided by how many sins you committed in your life, even though you had been forgiven by God through a priest.

But it was also a place where you suffered for your sins. I often wondered what they did to you in Purgatory. Suffering did not seem very nice to me and that made me go to confession. I remember going into those confessional boxes trying to disguise my voice.

"Bless me father for I have sinned. It has been six weeks since my last confession," I lied.

"Jeff Mills, you remind me of a dirty public lavatory!" the Priest replied.

I always thought if I get into that confessional box just before I die, then my chances of going to heaven would be pretty good.

The persistence of my friend, Paul, finally got to me. I was getting tired and felt like kicking his head in. One day I told him I was ready to visit his so-called home group. I was still not able to walk very far, but I could drive (even though I should not really have been driving with so many drugs inside of me). On the 6th of December 1990, I arrived at the house unaware that my life was about to change forever.

At the last minute, I thought of not going in but Paul was there tapping on my car window, with a big grin on his face.

"Too late, I am trapped now," I panicked. I gave him a sickly grin and with some difficulty got out of my car.

"Maybe if I pretend to faint, I won't have to see his peculiar friends," I reasoned. But that was not about to happen. Paul grabbed my arm and almost dragged me into the house. I met some other Germans and an American couple named Joel and Debbie Hollingsworth. I found out later they were missionaries to Germany.

"Hey Englishman, good to meet you, man!" came the roaring voice of Joel as he squeezed me in a bear hug. He was not aware of my back problem which now worsened one hundred percent! Somehow, I managed to find a chair and flopped down into it, my face contorted with pain. I watched this strange group singing worship songs in English and German with their hands raised high in the air. At first, I thought this must be an aerobics exercise they were practicing before realizing they were seriously into worshipping Jesus Christ.

Each one of those songs spoke about the love of Christ and what He had done for them. Afterwards Joel read some verses from the Bible and I continued to think what a funny group of people they were. This was not like the Catholic Church where you didn't dare make a noise in case you woke God up. He was stuck in a small box on the altar.

But then Joel read something that made me feel as though a dagger pierced my heart.

> *"For God so loved the world, that He gave His only son, and that whomsoever believes in Him will not die but have eternal life"*
> *John 3:16.*

That verse stirred something in me.

Right there and then in the kitchen of this American missionary, I began to cry like a baby. I couldn't stop, and I did not know what was happening. Tears were pouring out of me and my whole body was shaking. The startling truth of what Jesus Christ had done for me – personally for me – and also for the world, shocked me to the core of my being.

How could God give up His only Son to die for all our sins? Why hadn't the Catholic Church taught us these things? They never explained that thousands of people who thought they were going to heaven, were in fact going to hell. I began to understand I had to flee from sin and run to Jesus.

> *"Run from sexual sin! No other sin as clearly affects the body as this one does. For sexual immorality is a sin against your own body" 1 Corinthians 6:18.*

They asked me if I understood I was a sinner. Was I willing to ask Christ for His forgiveness for my sins, and accept Jesus Christ as my Lord and Savior?

Immediately I said, "Yes!"

They laid their hands on my head as I asked Jesus to forgive me for all I had done. I finally realized what a sinner I was, and that I was hanging over the very pits of hell.

I cried out to Jesus, "Forgive me, Jesus, forgive me! I believe You died on the cross for all my sins, and that You arose again on the third day so I too could have eternal life with You in heaven."

At that moment I knew I was saved from hell. I felt all the dirt come off my body and I was a new person.

> *"This means that anyone who belongs to Christ has become a new person. The old life is gone; a new life has begun!" 2 Corinthians 5:17.*

I had at last received Him into my life! Glory to God in the highest! I was told all the angels in heaven were rejoicing over me and my name was being written in heaven in a great big Book of Life.

A lot more patting on my back and bear hugs from these people, and I didn't even feel any pain as my tears continued to flow without embarrassment. Over a few cups of coffee, they shared more about Jesus Christ and the Gospel. I don't even like coffee, but I was so ecstatic it could have been water for all I cared. I didn't want to leave. I had never heard so much about Jesus in all my time as a Roman Catholic.

"Please Lord don't let this end," I prayed.

They asked me to pray and I found that very awkward. Everyone was staring at me as I prayed and thanked God for this wonderful evening, and asked him for forgiveness for threatening my friend Paul every day for months. There was laughter all around and I was beaming from ear to ear.

Chapter 7

The New Life

I had never felt happier in my life as I left to go home. Paul invited me to the church he attended in the German city of Wuppertal the following Sunday.

I sang all the way home. I had never felt so good. When I entered my house, Christa didn't know what to make of me. I was beaming from ear to ear even though I was still suffering with my back problems. She asked what happened, and I replied, "I have accepted Jesus Christ as my Lord and Savior."

"What have you got yourself into now?" Christa reacted. "Have you been seeing those Jehovah Witnesses again?"

Over the next few days, she saw many changes in me. She had been trying to get me to change for years! Curious, she came with me to the Wuppertal Free Evangelical church. It was nothing like the churches she or I had been to previously. Here were happy people. They greeted me as a brother, even though they didn't know me. People spoke normally and not in whispers like I was used to in the Roman Catholic Church.

The worship group began to sing. The musicians played guitars, drums and violins. There was not a church organ in site! People raised both their hands to worship God. I had never seen such worship in my entire life. The place was alive with what I learned later was the presence of the Holy Spirit.

A man with long hair came onto the platform and began to preach with such power, I could hardly stand. I later found out his name was Uwe Schaefer, a charismatic pastor and a man of authority. As he shared the Word of God, I broke down in tears, sobbing, and not really caring what others thought. I almost expected someone to shove a bottle of milk in my mouth and say, "Shut up!"

Pastor Uwe Schafer came to pray for me after the service. I was still weeping and a puddle formed on the ground. He smiled and told me God was moving in my life and not to worry about the tears. Great, I thought, He will even wipe the puddle of tears up! If I followed Jesus, he continued, the Lord would use me in more powerful ways.

"Powerful ways for what?" I wondered! I had no idea what he was talking about. I was just so happy. My world was changing to the fast lane and I didn't know if I was going to survive it. Would everything come crashing down soon?

A few weeks later Christa, out of curiosity, started to come to the home groups and on 6th January 1991 – the Feast of the Three Kings – she gave her life to Christ, also with many tears. Earlier I had found Christa to be a very hard type of character, and I watched God transforming her into a soft and beautiful rose.

Later we became members of a much smaller church closer to where we lived. The Joshua Church had been founded in Dortmund a few months earlier by an American missionary couple, Tim and Sandy Carter. Another American missionary couple, Joel and Debbie Hollingsworth, worked with this couple as co-pastors.

I had met Joel when I received Christ into my life and we decided this was the church for us. It was a brand-new church and had about twenty-five members. It was also very close to my favorite football club, Borussia Dortmund. Little did I know we would be very involved in seeing this church grow much larger.

Over the next few months, Christa and I were so hungry to learn more about Jesus Christ. Many nights I read my Bible under the bed covers just like a little child. We went to every meeting, wherever Christ was being preached. There was a fire burning in both of us and we didn't want it to go out.

Why didn't someone share this wonderful message with me years ago? Surely if we Christians have the answer to eternal life with God, then we should be out on the streets every single day? How could we possibly allow thousands to die and go to hell without knowing about Jesus? It reminded me of a doctor walking into a ward of cancer patients screaming in pain. He had the cure for cancer, but was too busy with his studies to tell them so they died. That is just the same for us. Knowing we have the answer to eternal life and not sharing it because we are too involved in things of the world, so people die and go to hell. How could we possibly not share Christ? Little did I know that soon God was going to use both Christa and myself in the area of missions and evangelism.

One night I was reading my Bible and I came across the following verse:

> *"By His stripes we are healed" (Psalm 53:3). Then I read:*
> *"He personally carried our sins in his body on the cross so that we can be dead to sin and live for what is right. By his wounds you are healed"* 1 Peter 2:24.

It was incredible to read Jesus died for ALL our sins and ALL our sicknesses. Wow! I got more and more excited.

"Christa, I believe that verse is for me as well! God wants to heal me!" I shouted excitedly. That night I prayed and asked Jesus to heal me right there. Nothing happened, but I was not dismayed. I thought maybe He is busy healing others and I have to get in line. At some of the meetings I went to, I saw people getting healed and each time I went up and asked for prayer.

"Well, it's got to happen or else this Bible is telling lies," I exclaimed to Christa. "God has told us to walk in faith and that is what I am doing right now."

> *"You don't have enough faith" Jesus told them. "I tell you the truth, if you had faith even as small as a mustard seed, you could say to this mountain, 'Move from here to there,' and it would move. Nothing would be impossible" Matthew 17:20.*

Another night I woke up suddenly and I saw a bright white figure standing by my bedside. He was at least ten-foot tall, This was an angel sent by God and he suddenly lifted up my whole body in his arms. My back was paining while he held me, and then he spoke in a quiet, gentle voice. "I am going to bring complete healing to your back and use you for my Kingdom!" With that, he laid me down again on my bed.

I believe this actually happened and it was not a dream. I woke Christa and asked, "Did you not see that figure?" No, she had not seen anything, but I knew God was speaking to me and now I could not get back to sleep. The next few nights I hoped the angel would come back. I prayed and prayed, "Lord speak to me again, please!"

God's timing is not always our timing, but it is perfect. I remembered reading the following Psalm:

> *"For you, a thousand years are as a passing day, as brief as a few night hours" Psalm 90:4.*

A few months later, my son Jon who lived in England wanted to visit me in Germany. On the way back from the airport I had told him about all the changes in my life and he looked at me very strangely. The next day I took him to a meeting in Dusseldorf where Pastor Peter Riedl had invited many ministers to a pre-founding of a church he was just starting. Eric Cowley, an international evangelist from the USA, was ministering and preached about the Jesus who heals today. If my memory serves me right, he spoke about the man with leprosy:

> *"A man with leprosy came and knelt in front of Jesus, begging to be healed." If you are willing, you can heal me and make*

> *me clean," he said. Moved with compassion, Jesus reached out and touched him. "I am willing," he said. "Be healed!" Mark 1:40-41*

It was just the message I wanted to hear! Afterwards he invited the sick to come forward for prayer and I shuffled my way from the back of the room to the front. I remember the evangelist shouting to me, "Stop right there, young man in the red cardigan!"

Well, I was the only man in a red cardigan and believed myself to be a young man, so I stopped. He continued, "God wants to heal your back right now."

"Yes," I said, "I know!"

He laid his hands on my head. I felt power like electricity passing right through my body, and a warm glow I had never felt before. Over one hundred people saw a miracle happening that night, many of them pastors, including my soon-to--be director of Globe Mission, Andreas Pestke.

All the pain immediately left me and I was able to bend, run, and dance. I cried tears of joy as people clapped and joined in praising God for what He had done.

Eric Cowley said, "I came all the way from the United States to pray for the Germans and an Englishman receives a miracle and gets healed!"

God certainly does have a sense of humor and I was so glad I had gone to the meeting.

Jon, my son, watched this happen and as we hurried home to share with Christa, he said he could hardly believe what had happened. This opened the door for me to share about Jesus Christ.

Christa was over the moon to see me healed. She had to do so much for me and now I could do everything myself.

Jon spoke with me and said, "Dad, if God can heal you, He can also heal me. If I get healed, I will become a Christian."

"God doesn't work that way, Jon," I replied. "If you accept Christ into your life first I will pray for you and God will heal you."

Jon had a greenstick fracture to his wrist a few years earlier and it had bothered him all this time. After I had shared the Gospel with him, he agreed to receive Christ into his life and then I prayed for him. He was instantly healed and nearly fell off his chair with excitement!

I give God all the glory for what He has done in me.

Chapter 8

My First Mission Trip

The following Sunday I shared my testimony in our church about what God had done for me. They saw me jumping up and down and dancing and they joined in with my happiness. They were amazed that only a week earlier I shuffled into church with my broken body, and now here I was feeling twenty years younger and ready to do a marathon!

I had been a Christian only six months and I wanted to do more for God. I had such a hunger and thirst to know Him better. God saw my desire and that was soon to happen!

One evening we were at a home group. A visiting English preacher gave me a small piece of torn paper with an address in Romania.

"I believe God would like you to go this address!" he said.

I was taken aback, not fully understanding this was directly from the Lord.

"Go!" said my wife.

I made arrangements immediately to visit the pastor mentioned on that piece of paper. He lived in the town of Constanta in Romania. My Pastor, Carsten Buck, always encouraging, gave me the go-ahead to make this visit.

A week later with the help of my wife Christa, I loaded up my car with food and clothes and started off on a journey that was to fully test my faith. The trip took three days and passed through three countries. As I drove through Hungary singing worship songs, I was stopped by a policeman who said I had been speeding and had to pay a fine.

"How fast was I driving?" I asked him.

"Too fast!" he said.

I knew this could not be true, and I looked enquiringly at him.

"I have a family to feed and need some money," he said eventually. I smiled and gave him a "donation" for my crime.

I had to wait ten hours at the border of Hungary and Romania to cross over. It was night and I was very exhausted. I could not sleep for fear of losing my place in the line. There were some very rough-looking people around, so I kept my car door locked. One policeman looked at me and then the food in the car, and put his finger across his throat. I think he was telling me I was not going to live, there were many bandits in Romania, and it was dangerous driving alone!

If ever there was a time I needed the Lord, it was now. For a few seconds, I thought of turning around and going home, but I opened my bible and read from Isaiah 40:11:

> *"Like a shepherd he takes care of his flock. He gathers the lambs in his arms. He carries them in his arms. He gently helps the sheep and their lambs." Now I felt safe enough to continue my journey.*

This was an exciting adventure for me, but there was worse to come! As night came, I looked in my rear-view mirror and noticed a van following me with four or five rough-looking men inside. I accelerated the car but they continued to follow me. I was driving over 120 kilometers and knew I was breaking the speed limit.

After about five minutes of a really fast-speed chase, I realized they truly were after me and drove even faster, praying and asking the

Lord to help me. Suddenly in the middle of nowhere, standing right in the middle of the road I saw a policeman with a young boy of about eight years old by his side. He signaled for me to stop and, believe me, it was a great pleasure to obey him! I skidded to a halt, smoke pouring from the tires of my car. The van following me did a quick U-turn and disappeared in the opposite direction.

I wound my car window down, expecting to get a ticket. The policeman did not say a word, but took my map off the passenger seat and pointed to a town I was making for that night. He obviously wanted a lift, so they both got into the back of the car, still without a word. Later I looked in my rearview mirror and saw they were both sound asleep.

I put the car safety-lock on and felt a lot safer. God has answered my prayer!

> *"And we are confident that he hears us whenever we ask for anything that pleases him. And since we know he hears us when we make our requests, we also know that he will give us what we ask for"* 1 John 5:14-15.

Strange really, because friends had told me there were many bandits about and I was not to stop, even for policemen because they too would rob you. But with this man and his son, I knew God had helped me.

Three hours later, after a grueling trip over winding treacherous roads and through the mountains with fog making it hard to see, I rolled into the town about midnight.

Suddenly the policeman tapped me on the back, pointing to a hotel. I stopped the car to let them out, turning around to say goodbye. They had both disappeared! The doors were still locked!

My hair stood up when I realized I had given a lift to angels. I had put the safety lock on all the doors so they could not have got out. Not only that, it was within seconds after I had stopped the car that I had turned around.

The Bible says in Hebrews 13:2

> *"Don't forget to show hospitality to strangers, for some who have done this have entertained angels without realizing it!"*

I wondered if anyone would believe me when I returned to Germany, but I did not care as I knew God was taking care of me. Wow! So much action and I had not even arrived at my destiny.

That night I stayed in the hotel where I had stopped. I was very hungry, but they told me they had only a little food and I accepted it with gratitude. They also gave me a bottle of wine!

They were concerned about my car being parked in front of the hotel and said it was almost certain it would get stolen. Well God had taken care of me so far, so I asked the Lord to put his angels around my car and the next morning it was still there!

"Don't be afraid, for I am with you," I sensed the Spirit of God minister to me. The Word of God says in Isaiah 41:10:

> *"Don't be discouraged, for I am your God. I will strengthen you and help you. I will hold you up with my victorious right hand."*

I had a slight headache that morning and wondered whether it was the bottle of wine I had with my dinner! But no, I had taken one sip and spat it out. It tasted like something I never wanted to taste again!

Chapter 9

Constanta and Miracles

At last I arrived in Constanta on the Black Sea and met George and his family, my hosts. I later found out George was a great man of God. His life had been threatened a number of times, but he continued winning people to the Lord. The family had prepared a big meal for me and as tired as I was, we celebrated late into the night even though we hardly understood one another. They were so happy to receive all the food that I had brought, but they took a special interest in the toilet rolls! After using their bathroom, I understood why. All I found was newspaper!

The next morning, we were walking towards the church and I could hear the choir singing so beautifully. I remarked to George how nice the music was, and then asked him what he was going to preach about. His reply made my legs turn to jelly.

"Brother Jeff, **you** are preaching!" came the reply.

"What!" I answered; "I have never preached in my life, I can't do that" was my stuttered answer.

"Brother Jeff the Lord told me that he has sent you here to pray for our sick people and to lift us up, they are all awaiting you."

As I entered the building I was hoping no one would notice I was sweating, not with the heat, but with fear! My stomach was turning over and I wanted to lean on George. Maybe I would pretend to faint and then I would not have to preach!

The church was packed full; people had come from other churches to hear my message that I had not prepared. Should I run away now, get into my car and drive back to Germany were my thoughts at this moment? Maybe I would go to the bathroom and then climb through the window. But no, I was trapped and George was grinning at me and patting me on my back.

"Lord take me now, please take me!" I was praying under my breath, but He wasn't listening, or maybe He was and was just testing me.

As I stepped up on the platform after being introduced, the people stood clapping at me.

"Oh Lord, only you can help me!" was my prayer.

With legs shaking I said a quick and silent prayer to the Lord to give me strength, and suddenly I felt strong again. I knew I had to rely on the presence of the Holy Spirit, and proclaim Jesus Christ and the scandal of the cross.

I started to share my testimony of my miracle healing to my back and also about the angels that had saved my life. I continued to share some verses on healing and told them it was for them as well. All of a sudden people started coming forward for their healings and miracles. I told the Lord that He was now in charge and that I was just His servant.

"He must increase and I must decrease" John 3:30.

I began to lay my hands on the sick, some were thrown to the floor and others began to shake. One lady who had one leg shorter than the other by at least 6 inches pulled the leg support off and started to dance screaming "Hallelujah, hallelujah!" She began running around the church, falling sometimes as she had never ever walked on two even feet ever before in her life. Later I heard one woman was healed of brain cancer. I stood there weeping, yet again, God had not let me down.

> *"They will be able to handle snakes with safety, and if they drink anything poisonous, it won't hurt them. They will be able to place their hands on the sick, and they will be healed." Mark 16:18*

The next day we visited some villages where I continued to pray for the sick. I actually saw demons flee out of women and other people healed.

> *"Heal the sick, raise the dead, cure those with leprosy, ana cast out demons. Give as freely as you have received!" Matthew 10:8*

One elderly lady came up to me and began to pray and then give a prophetic word. George translated it, and she had said that I would be sent onto the mission field to work with dark-skinned people. The very next day another woman gave the same prophecy. I automatically thought of Africa, but no, God had other plans that I was soon to learn about. The thought of Christa or me being chased and eaten by a lion terrified me! ....and probably her!

Soon I had to return to Germany and there were many tears shed by the Romanian people, weeping they hugged me, and me weeping too I hugged them. Some gave me gifts which I treasure to this date. The trip was over too soon for me, and I wanted to stay longer but I also wanted to return to my wife Christa. My journey back to Germany went without incident except for the border guards who seemed to want a bribe off of me. I know someone had told me that it was not Christian-like to do such a thing, I played ignorant and they eventually allowed me through.

> *"And you shall take no bribe: for the bribe blinds the wise, and perverts the words of the righteous" Exodus 23:8.*

Chapter 10

Back to Romania

The following Sunday, back in Germany, excitedly I shared in our church service about my adventure in Romania. I told them about all the miracles I saw and demons fleeing as I shouted for them to release the Gypsies in the name of Jesus Christ. As I shared I saw people shaking their heads when I spoke about angels and miracles.

"These people don't believe me because I am such a young Christian!" I thought.

"You don't believe me, do you?" I challenged them.

There were smiles from the congregation! There and then, I decided, to take a group from our church to Romania later in the year.

This time twenty-two members of the church traveled with me by aircraft. It was hilarious! I still remember to this day the look on the face of my friend, Pastor Joel Hollingsworth. He looked terrified. The plane was an old Russian aircraft, painted over, with the Romanian flag pasted on it. I am sure the wheels of the plane were threadbare!

I was sat next to a man who was smoking. I was in a non-smoking chair and I asked the attendant if he would tell the man to put his cigarette out.

"Sir," he said, "you are in a non-smoking chair and he is in a smoking chair!"

This really was hilarious! He was sitting right next to me! I wanted to use the lavatory during the trip, but discovered one was out of order. Now even I was getting scared, wondering what the state of the engines was. I didn't dare to look out of the window at them!

Over the next few hours, the aircraft chugged its way to Romania. Many of us were praying for us to arrive safely.

I was keen to get to work in Romania sharing the Gospel. How anyone could live without knowing Jesus Christ was beyond me. Yet there are millions in the world who are blind, just like I had been.

We hired a hall capable of seating about two thousand people and placed a huge plastic advert on the building. It boldly advertised the up-and-coming evangelistic outreach. Sadly, by the next day it had been pulled down. I was not too worried as word soon got around the town that people from the West were here.

Joel Hollingsworth managed to get a Swedish Christian Rock Group to play at the meetings. I had seen a picture of this group in Germany. They all had long hair and some wore black leather jeans. I really did not want them to come and had prayed that they would cancel. Joel was praying that they **would** come! God heard Joel's prayers and not mine!

The next day they arrived in their own bus! Out stepped this man with an enormous amount of hair and, of course, wearing black jeans. Then another, and another.

"Father, what have I done to have this group?" I whispered under my breath in shock. But within a couple of hours I actually got to like them!

"The Lord does not look at the things man looks at. Man looks at the outward appearance, but the Lord looks at the heart"
1 Samuel 16:7.

God is so good. That night the group started playing. They had a 12-foot black cross with red lights all around it and many pastors would not come into the building. They stood outside and said we were from the devil.

That night the healings began, and devils were cast out of people. The pastors heard about the miracles, healings and casting out of demons that were happening as the team ministered, and so the second night they all came in. By the third night, the hall was full and they were dancing and clapping along with us. It was a great week with wonderful results.

Chapter 11

Unsettled

A week after returning to Germany I was extremely unsettled in my spirit. I was hungry to do more for the Lord and spent much time in prayer and reading the Word of God.

"Father you sent an angel to me and said You would use me," I cried out to the Lord one night. "Two people gave me the same prophecy. Come on, Lord, tell me what you want me to do!"

A few weeks later Christa and I attended a meeting where Loren Cunningham, the founder of YWAM (Youth With a Mission) was preaching. Half-way through the message his interpreter lost his voice and my dear wife, Christa, stood in and interpreted for Loren Cunningham.

I had heard so much about this great man of God and how he had moved in faith most of his life, and this is what I wanted to do as well. I was so hungry for more of the Lord.

As he preached, Loren Cunningham spoke about a day the Lord told him to go to the airport and fly to Hawaii. He obeyed, but still wondered how he would fly to Hawaii when he had no money and no ticket. At the airport with his small suitcase, he stood in line at the ticket counter still wondering what God would do. The line was long. There was one person ahead of him when a lady came up to him and shoved an envelope into his hands.

"God told me to give you this," she said.

In the envelope was his return ticket to Hawaii. God is so good, isn't He?!

Loren Cunningham spoke of the many more miracles he has experienced, and now has the headquarters of YWAM in Hawaii. All this happened by walking in faith.

I was in the fast lane now and certainly learning so much about this wonderful God of ours and what He was doing with those who walked in faith.

That day we also met two Americans – Ron and Pat Kelly, the directors of Living Water Ministries in Guatemala, Central America. Their ministry involved feeding programs for the poor children in the mountains and other areas.

"Jeff, why don't you go to Guatemala for a few weeks and hear what God is saying?" Christa said. "Ask Ron or Pat Kelly if you could go there?"

Ron put up an "Adopt-a-Child" display as they were hoping the German people would sponsor a child. Their vision was to break into different countries with this program. The only problem was that in their ministry, nobody spoke German.

I was a bit hesitant as I walked up to Ron and Pat, but I found them very warm-hearted. Ron greeted me with a bear hug! I noticed they had already produced the flyers in German. That was walking in faith again!

"Hello Ron, hello Pat, I am Jeff Mills. I live here in Germany with my German wife, Christa."

"Ah Jeff, I heard about you and your miracle!" said Ron.

That threw me off balance for a second, but I continued, "Is it possible I could come to Guatemala for a few weeks? I want to hear what God is doing with me."

"Sure, you can come, no problem," Pat responded.

I was so grateful to them and also very excited.

Over the next few weeks, I spent a lot of time praying and finding out as much information as I could, while also trying to raise funds for our church. I was grateful once again that my pastor was behind me going.

One person nearly put me off by saying, "Jeff, do you realize there is a civil war going on in Guatemala?"

"Oh, my goodness!" I thought to myself, "Maybe I will get killed or kidnapped."

But in my prayer time, I had true peace and so did Christa. I began to get my clothes together, excitedly wondering what was going to happen whilst I was there.

The first few nights I found it hard to sleep but I soon settled down. I had to get a visa from the Guatemalan Embassy and that went extremely smoothly.

Chapter 12

My First Trip to Guatemala

Christa took me to the airport in Dusseldorf and we had our farewell hugs and kisses. My trip to Guatemala was a weary, but exciting twenty-six hours. I flew via Madrid and Mexico and arrived in Guatemala at 11.30 pm local time.

I was glad to see Kelly's waiting for me, but sadly my luggage never arrived until three days later! I expected to see military everywhere, but everything seemed tranquil.

The next few weeks I was shown around the ministry and its many feeding programs in the mountains. Many of the Mayan indigenous lived there in really squalid conditions. My heart went out to the hundreds of children who came daily to the feeding programs. They all had with big smiles and big black sparkling eyes.

Here was I, a man who could not work with children, and God placed me in the middle of 5,000 of them! I spent hours watching these children gobble down their food and then go to Bible classes. My heart for children was changing very fast, and so the tears began to fall as well.

I attended church services in all of the ministry's churches spread over Guatemala, and the missionaries were always there to take me to them. There seemed to be church services every night! The music was loud, loud, loud, but the face of Jesus shone on these people. I saw many of them weeping openly on the floor, not caring about getting their clothes dirty. Others were prophesying, whilst demons were being cast out of still others. All at the same time! The glory of God was in all the churches and the people seemed so happy.

One evening I was at one of the church services. The missionaries and pastors were in a circle for a prayer and suddenly Ron asked me to step into the middle with another visiting pastor from the USA and prophesy over the people.

"Me? You sure you are talking to me, Ron?"

He sure was, but I just stood there as the other pastor began to pray over people. About five minutes later, the Lord spoke to me and I began to also lay hands on the people.

"The grass is greener where I am sending you," I spoke prophetically to Pastor Robin Garcia as I laid hands on him. I had never met him before. He wept because Ron Kelly had given him a similar word only one week earlier. I then laid my hand on a woman, whom I later found out was his wife. Ofelia, and gave had the same message! God is so amazing, isn't He?

I felt so frustrated not being able to communicate with the Guatemalans as I spoke no Spanish, except the word "gracias" – Thank you!

One afternoon, about four weeks after arriving in Guatemala, I was sitting in the ministry house in a dark corner so no one could see me and began to sob. I cried so loud the young Mayan girls who worked in the house heard me. They were so frightened, they ran to call Ron and Pat Kelly to come and see me.

I felt so embarrassed when I saw them staring at me, lying on the floor weeping so loudly. Here was an ex-soldier of twenty-three years' service for the Queen of England, weeping. Veterans are tough; they don't cry! But believe me, there was a puddle on the floor just next to me and it wasn't from Kelly's dog!

What was God doing with me! Ron and Pat Kelly assured me this was not unusual, and explained that many people wept openly after seeing what was happening in the ministry in Guatemala. They prayed for me, and afterward, sheepishly, I returned to my bedroom.

In the late hours of that night, I awoke to hear a voice speaking to me. Looking around, I could see no one. It was then I realized the Lord was speaking! Excitedly, I took my notebook and clearly heard the Lord say He wanted both Christa and me in Guatemala as missionaries. Once more, tears flooded my eyes as I wept in His presence, thanking Him and talking back to Him.

Suddenly the realization struck me. What about Christa? Maybe she would not want to come? God had not spoken with her and this might affect our marriage!

I prayed earnestly to the Lord that He would speak to Christa before I flew back to Germany. Abba Father was not to let me down!

The day before my return to Germany, I shared with Ron and Pat what I had heard from the Lord, hoping that they would not laugh at me. I was surprised at their reaction.

"Jeff, we have been praying now for three months for God to send us a German-speaking person and an administrator as we have just broken into Germany with our ministry," Ron said.

Isn't God good? He moves us around like chess pieces. It was with a heavy heart that I left Guatemala. Tears welled up in my eyes as I said goodbye to the many new friends I had met. But I knew I would be returning one day.

The Father had made that clear to me.

Chapter 13

The Preparation

Back in Germany, Christa was not surprised. She had already heard from the Lord.

"O Father, You are so wonderful. You have not let me down," I prayed to Him.

And so the first preparations began with a talk with our pastor - Carsten Buck.

"God always takes my best people." He smiled. "You have my blessing!"

Carsten was an inspiration to me and I considered him a true man of God. He allowed me to preach in the church on occasions and guided me many times. I believe without his teachings, we would never have been in Guatemala and I truly have a lot to thank him for, together with his beautiful wife, Marie.

A further interview was arranged with Pastor Brad Thurston, an American missionary and the director of a newly formed mission organization called, Globe Europe (now Globe Mission) located in the town of Wesel, Germany.

Somewhat nervous, we were warmly welcomed by various members of the staff from Globe Europe, and especially by Janet Thurston with her lovely Scottish accent.

"Don't worry," she said as we were led into the director's office. "God is with you."

I will never forget those words of encouragement. I found out later she truly has a wonderful gift of encouraging people.

Brad also made us very welcome. After many questions about our lives, he explained what it cost to be a missionary in another country. It meant everything – giving up our family, our friends, and even our house.

We really did live in a beautiful house. It was the envy of the village, overlooking the village pond with its own creek running through the garden.

I was so excited as we talked, but was soon came down to earth when Brad Thurston explained we had to raise our own funds from various churches.

"What? I only know two churches!" I said desperately.

But Brad explained that if God wanted us in Guatemala, then doors would open for us. And God came through for us. Our funds were raised very quickly from churches we never even knew existed. I was discovering that when you are in the will of God, no man could stop you doing what He has planned.

The following verse came to my mind:

> *"For I know the plans I have for you, declares the LORD, plans to prosper you and not to harm you, plans to give you hope and a future" Jeremiah 29:11.*

I wrote to seventy-two churches in the UK and only two replied. They were both from Scotland and have supported us for many years. All our other supporting churches were in Germany

Nine months later we were ready to leave Germany for our new home in Guatemala. A special sending-out church service was held and Pastor Uwe Schafer was the invited guest to pray for us, along with

Pastor Carsten Buck. There were many tears were shed that day, including ours.

We had held a sale of all our personal belongings that we could not take with us. Our boxes were sent ahead of us and we left Dusseldorf Airport with two suitcases each.

Once more, after another really long journey changing aircraft twice, Ron and Pat Kelly met us at the airport. This time our baggage arrived.

Before being allowed into the country, there was a lot of paperwork still to be completed at the airport. Guatemala had been in a state of civil war for over 25 years.

Over the next few weeks, it seemed almost impossible to get our shipped boxes out of the warehouse without paying a bribe. I was soon to learn the country was incredibly corrupt. I refused to pay any bribe and asked the Lord to take care of any problem that might arise.

> *"For the king trusts in the LORD. The unfailing love of the Most High will keep him from stumbling" Psalm 21:7.*

For the twentieth time, I returned to the airport with a Guatemalan driver in his pickup. This time the boxes were there.

"But you will have to pay for the time they have been in storage," I was told.

"How many days have they been in storage?" asked my Guatemalan driver.

"Fifty-eight days," came the reply.

"What?" I shouted! "That's exactly how many days we have been in Guatemala!"

So, the boxes had actually come on the same aircraft we were on! Each time we came to ask for the boxes, they said no – and now they wanted us to pay for the fifty-eight days storage!

My driver told me to wait outside, and to this day I do not know what happened, but our boxes were loaded immediately.

Chapter 14

Some of the History of Guatemala

To fully understand the conditions missionaries have to work under in Guatemala, one needs to know a bit of its history.

Guatemala is a country in Central America with a population of 16 million people and is situated in between Mexico, Belize, and El Salvador. Seven million of the people live in the Capital of Guatemala, mainly in squalid conditions. Its main language is Spanish and there are 23 different dialects. mainly spoken by the Mayan Indigenes who are the majority in this land, but also the poorest. The remainder are the Latino and of these only one percent are rich.

The country is rich in color because it has only one climate – Spring. It is therefore called, "The Land of Eternal Spring." Flowers and vegetation abound in this rich, warm, fertile land.

But it also has a dark history with a long 30-year civil war. Over 30,000 lost their lives before it ended in 1997. In 1976 over 25,000 people lost their lives in an earthquake that struck in the middle of the night on 4 February. A further 100,000 were injured and lost their homes.

Even today, the majority of families live in poverty and the government has no answer to this problem. More than 60% of children die of malnutrition and other diseases. This happens mainly among the Mayans. Many of them believe visiting a doctor or hospital means dying, and they are correct because they often come too late to be helped!

Even though the country has almost fifty-percent born-again Christians, poverty is rife and the crime rate is very high. Many people turn to crime because the country has no welfare system. It is a case of work, die, or become a thief.

At the time of writing, three Presidents who served whilst we have been here ended up in prison for corruption. Many of the acaldies (mayors) are also in prison. Recently half the previous government ended up in prison, along with six of the last police chiefs who decided to join them!

The prisons are a time bomb with so much overcrowding, and many prisoners have been murdered during riots. This is why there is a great need for the Gospel of Jesus Christ to be shared with the lost.

One time I visited a prison and shared Christ with the gangs. Some received Christ into their lives, but soon I was stopped from entering the prison, which saddened me. But the message has been received and the rest is up to the Holy Spirit.

There are also numbers of bus and taxi drivers, and even shopkeepers, who refuse to pay for "protection" and are murdered. In this country, it's pay or die!

Catholicism is mixed with Mayan witchcraft and this can be openly seen in some of the churches in the mountains. The Mayans worship a wooden idol called Mashimon, or by another name – Saint-Simon. When there is sickness or alcoholics in their families, they will call on the Shaman or witchdoctor and are required to bring a bottle of alcohol with them. The witchdoctor then carries out ritual chanting songs, dancing whilst pouring alcohol into the mouth of Mashimon – and into his own mouth! I am sure these witchdoctors enjoy all the free booze! The Mayans have a great fear of this "god" as sometimes people do actually get healed or die.

During the Easter period, religious ceremonies are held in most towns and villages. The Catholics carry floats with the figures of Jesus, Joseph, and Mary, plus other saints. Sometimes it can take up to 100 men to carry one of these floats. They must pay a penance to carry out this ritual.

The people walk over carpets made of straw and flowers which have taken families many hours to make, and are ruined in just a few minutes. Families choose to go hungry in order to spend their money on these carpets

Thousands of people come from all over the world to watch the processions. Many hotels are booked one year in advance. Locals take advantage of this and rent out their rooms for hundreds of US dollars.

It is beautiful to see, but it is not of God and I am sure He weeps when he sees these evil rituals carried out each year. The Catholics here seem to worship Mary more than Jesus, and I have heard the Pope would like to make her equal with Jesus. If only they would understand that the Bible tells us we can only worship God.

In the last two weeks of Lent, Christa and I avoid driving into the town of Antigua, where she does nearly does her shopping. Although it is close to us, it is impossible to move because of the processions. I once got caught behind one procession and it took ninety minutes to make a journey of five minutes.

Chapter 15

The Learning Period

Before coming to Guatemala, we studied various books about what a missionary really was. Some of the books terrified me as I could not walk on water yet!

But something I learned from a quote by Henry Merritt Wriston impressed me. It was about the qualities one should have: *Work, Wealth, and Wisdom; preferably all three; but at least two of the three."* The 3W's as they are known, encompass much of what missionaries do, with one important addition – the Word of God.

I believe this to be the defining "W" for a missionary is the *Word of God*. The primary job of any missionary is to proclaim Jesus as Lord and Savior; to bring the Gospel, which is the Good News that Jesus came to provide forgiveness for our sins, to redeem us, and restore us to God.

1 Corinthians 15:1-4 teaches us that Christians are called to reach "all the nations" Matthew 28:19 compels us to bring the Gospel to those people who have not yet heard, and an essential part of that calling is to "Make disciples of all nations".

From this, I understand the calling of a missionary extends beyond merely sharing the Gospel. Salvation is the first step in the life of a Christian. Growing in knowledge and faith in Christ so as to become

His disciples is a process and one where a missionary plays an important role.

Jesus also calls on Christians to care physically for those is a need. James 1:27 is just one example:

> *"Religion that is pure and undefiled before God, the Father, is this: to visit orphans and widows in their affliction, and to keep oneself unstained from the world."*

Now I saw our calling a lot differently! This was not just widows and orphans, but anyone in need. In James:15-16 we read:

> *"If a brother or sister is poorly clothed and lacking in daily food, and one of you says to them, "Go in peace, be warmed and filled," without giving them these things needed for the body, what good is that?"*

Very clearly, God expects us to go beyond sharing the Good News of the Gospel by also assisting those in need in a very real and physical way. David Livingstone and Hudson Taylor were both amazing, world changing missionaries who used their skills as doctors, amongst other things, to serve those in the countries in which they were called.

These verses have helped Christa and me so much. Many times people have knocked on our front door asking for money, food, and medicines and we have always given it.

They tend to say, "Can we borrow some money? "But in reality, they mean, "Will you *give* me some money?"

Don Salvador, an elderly man in his eighties, used to come every Saturday morning and sweep the front of our house. In return we gave him some money, and also on occasions clothes and empty tins. Sometimes he brought us a gift of some mangos. At the time of writing, Don Salvador has just passed away.

One of the other W's is *Work*. Missionary work is 24/7. It is preaching, teaching, and discipling day in and day out. Believe me, as a missionary I have cleaned toilets, mopped floors, helped build houses, and cooked. Matthew 23:11 says, *"The greatest among you shall be your servant."*

Jesus laid out His example for us in John 13 when He washed His disciple's feet and told them they should follow His example. If washing the feet of those He was discipling was not beneath our Lord, is there any job that is beneath us in the service of those we are called to disciple?

One evening at a church service I felt called to wash one person's feet, but when I asked him to come forward he hesitated. Later I found out why! His socks were stuck to his feet! I am sure he must have worn the same socks for a year. I peeled off his sock and his feet stank! With tears in my eyes, I washed both his feet, even though I felt like throwing up. God was testing me!

The next "W" is *Wisdom*. Missionaries are called to have a solid knowledge of Scripture and be grounded in true doctrine. Now here was where my problem lay my problem because I was not grounded in the Word. I was always interested in studying the Word, but there were parts I did not understand. I hold no degrees but I believe the Lord saw my willingness to learn.

I have been humbled on many occasions where a Guatemalan has taught me many new things from the Bible. So, my wisdom has grown over the years in Guatemala.

Wealth is the last "W". Now this one makes me want to fall over laughing! For the past twenty-three years, we have worked with limited resources, at times having to beg or scrounge for support and donations. Many of the projects have been completed by sheer faith.

However, we do have connections with family, friends, and donors in four different countries. Each year prices rise steeply, but our monthly donations have remained the same. Despite asking more people to support our work, the same donors seem to keep us going.

Yes, we live by faith, going ahead where God leads us. Perhaps more than the wealth of finances, what we have is a wealth of faith –

the belief and knowledge that if God has called us to do something, He will provide. Our job is simply to obey.

Chapter 16

The Fun Begins

Very soon after our arrival in Guatemala, we found a small house to rent not far from the ministry house. We lived out of our suitcases for two months while we waited for our boxes to arrive. We were quite amazed to find how easy it is to live on small resources.

Susana was our first muchacha (maid). She not only cleaned the house, but also made the midday meals, always inviting herself to lunch! One day she put a plate of chicken in front of me. I saw two eyes staring at me! And there were the feet of the chicken! Christa had to spend some time with her explaining what Europeans eat.

Susana often shared how hard life was bringing up three children, so we always gave her a bit extra at the end of the month. Years later, when I was in the local hospital, one of the nurses asked if I recognized her.

"No," I said.

"I am the youngest child of your maid, Susana, she told me.

Wow! I was amazed how fast time went. I was so proud this young girl had managed to study, even though her mother earned hardly anything.

In between Spanish school, we went to the Sunday services in six of the ministry's churches spread around Guatemala. Our hearts went out to the children and adults. They sing with all their might, many out of tune, but to God it is beautiful.

I began to feel very frustrated because the services never seemed to start on time. Some started as much as half-an-hour late. This was a culture shock to both of us. We were soon to learn that relationships were more important than time. If people were having a conversation, they would finish it before turning up for church services. Also, many people did not have watches. When they heard the first song, then only did they start to get ready.

Culture shock continued for the first year. It was not unusual for a Guatemalan Christian to tell a lie to a missionary. They just wanted to keep us happy! Many came to our house asking for money to buy medicines for their sick children or parents. It was a long time before we discovered they showed us the same receipt for medicine over and over again.

One day one woman asked if we could help pay for her grandmother's funeral. I gladly gave some money to her, but a few weeks later she came knocking on my door again asking for money

"Why do you need it?" I asked her.

"It's for my sick grandmother," she said with a sad expression.

Wait a moment, she died four weeks ago!

On another occasion, a lady asked me for money to buy a false leg for her sister. Not to be caught out this time, I told her I would like to come and pray for her sister.

"I am afraid Gringos are not allowed in the hospital," she said without blinking an eyelid. I prayed over this woman asking God to help her stop lying!

When we started work in the ministry, Ron Kelly put us in charge of the *Adopt-a-Child* administration program. He mentioned that many people complained they were not getting information about the children they were sponsoring. I was soon to find out why! At this time there was only one secretary in the office and there was no filing system and children's folders were stuck in different drawers. I could see everything for this young girl was way above her head.

One evening whilst she was not in the office, I broke open the filing cabinet and out rolled over 60 rolls of undeveloped film, as well as many unopened letters. The next day I sat this poor girl down. She sobbed loudly as she told me the job was just too much for her, but she was afraid of telling anyone. I assured her that her job was safe and that I would be speaking with the director and asking for two more staff to help. I would also be asking for new filing cabinets and extra desks.

The next ten months were spent developing the many rolls of film and changing the whole system of administration, which now had to include Germany. That was where Christa came in!

It also meant many trips to the mountains during a dangerous time with the guerillas and the army fighting each other. One of them took a shot at my car on one occasion! Before any journey to the mountains, I prayed from Psalm 91 for protection.

I was stopped by guerillas in some of the small towns, as well as by the police and army on many occasions. When they knew I was a missionary they would let me pass, but not before I gave them a tract.

High in the mountains on many occasion, we stayed in a compound. It looked like a fort out of the cowboy films. There was always a guard who carried a rifle that seemed too big for him, though I doubted it was even loaded.

During those years, there was no electricity for the people who lived in the area. Our "fort" had a generator which was switched off about 11.00pm each night. Until "lights out" we sat on the verandah and sometimes sang songs to the Lord. or just shared some of our experiences. It was a wonderful time and the presence of the Holy

Spirit was with us. It was not safe to go out alone, not only because of the guerillas, but also because hundreds of vampire bats flew very low in the pitch-black night!

One evening on the verandah I was sharing with one of the young pastors whose name was Goyo. I remarked how well he played the keyboard and was taken aback when he told me the following story.

"Brother Jeff, it was the missionaries who taught me about moving in faith, and also about the God of miracles. I was determined to play the keyboard. So one night I locked myself in the church building and told God I would not leave until I could play the keyboard. He did not let me down, and by the morning I was playing almost like a professional."

"I am not here to teach them; they are here to teach us!" I thought to myself as tears filled my eyes.

On occasions I would help in the clinic when groups came mainly from the USA and on occasions from the UK and Germany. I enjoyed working alongside the dentists and soon one of them taught me how to extract teeth. Wow! Now I was removing teeth of children, but it was not to end there.

As we were still in the middle of a civil war, I was involved in helping save the lives of two men who had been shot. Doctor Pablo asked for my help and I jumped to the occasion. Looking at blood never bothered me. Another time I helped him sew a finger back on a man. But my crowning glory was driving Doctor Pablo's wife to the hospital in a real ambulance! There I was tearing through the mountains with the sirens sounding and really enjoying this occasion.

"Hermano Jeff," Doctor Pablo shouted after me. "My wife is only pregnant, there is no need to sound the sirens!"

But I didn't hear him and loved it when the cars got out of the way for me! I think he was more worried about the many hairpin bends I had to navigate at top speed!

During my first year in Guatemala, I had an interpreter when I preached. His name was Amilcar Cabrera. He came from one of the ministry's churches which was situated on an old rubbish dump in Zone 5 of Guatemala City – known for its drug gang wars. When the police go into this area, they always go in large numbers!

Whenever I went to the church services there, I always took an extra shirt and towel as the worship was so powerful people outside the church building were often overcome by the power of the Holy Spirit.

Why the shirt and towel? There were so many people packed into the building that after a couple of hours of worship one would be sweating profusely!

Amilcar is another miracle from God. He learned the English language in one night! God can do anything if your faith is in line with His Word. This was all part of the Father's plan for Amilcar.

Today Amilcar has his own ministry. He sends Guatemalan missionaries to different parts of the Islamic world. God is so wonderful.

Groups from the USA often came to visit for ten-day periods. Some were as large as forty and we took turns looking after them. This was a great time of meeting other Christians and being able to show them the ministry and also life in Guatemala.

Each group was given a task, which could be painting, building, or just visiting families to pray for them. It was also time of meeting the children they sponsored. There were many tears when they came to face with their sponsored child and shared gifts with them and their families.

On the last night of their trip, the people shared what had changed in their lives during the ten days they were in Guatemala. Many could not speak for crying; even grown men sobbed. But I think what moved me most was listening to the youth when they realized just how well off they were in the USA, compared to these people who had nothing but Jesus in their lives.

Chapter 17

The Change

After four years, I felt that our time had come to an end with the ministry. At the same time, I did not feel we should leave Guatemala. I became very restless and on the advice of my dear wife Christa, I started to seek the Lord for an answer.

Once more, the Lord did not let me down and we left Living Water Ministries shortly thereafter. Ron and Pat Kelly were a blessing to us and we had learned so much from them. We are truly thankful for all they taught us.

My heart was for evangelism, for which I had been ordained as a minister in the time with the ministry. The way was now open, but I still needed to hear clearly from the Father. We spent a year being part of the Verbo (Word) Church in a town close by called Jocotenango. It was a time of refreshing for our bodies and spirits. On occasions, I preached the Word in this church and came to know a lot of new friends.

One day I was preparing to drive to Guatemala City. On the exit to the town, I saw a man thumbing for a lift. I really did not like stopping for anyone, but I felt a shove from God saying, "Give him a lift Jeff."

I stopped my car, wound down the window and asked him in my best Spanish where he wanted to go.

"I want to go to Guatemala City," he said in very good English.

"Jump in" I replied, "That's where I am going."

He introduced himself Marco Estrada. Later I found he was a Godly man, but it was difficult to work out exactly what he was involved in! It seemed he had his hand in everything.

It was during this time the Lord gave me the name for our ministry. It was to be called *Final Harvest Ministries*. God had put into me a great urgency to share the Gospel with as many people as possible and I believe this is why He introduced Marco Estrada to me.

Two days later, Marco introduced me to a man named Luis Pitch. He pastored a church in a town called San Pedro de Las Huertas. He asked me to hold an evangelistic campaign for him.

"Sure," I replied, "Just let me know when."

By this time I had purchased a large tent from the USA that could hold one hundred people and we held quite a few tent evangelism campaigns. I saw people saved and healed, but still felt this was not the place God planned for me to be.

A year later, I clearly heard from the Lord that our call was to work alongside a young pastor by the name of Abner Gomez. He had started a home group with some young people in the town of Parramoss. On the day I first met him and his wife Lolly, they both wept as we talked together.

Abner told me he had been praying to the Lord to send him some missionaries to help them start a church. Isn't God wonderful? For the next two years, we worked alongside them. We erected the tent in the back garden of our house and that was to be our church for the next nine months while we looked for another building. By this time we had over one hundred members.

Parramoss often lost its electricity and the town would be in darkness for two or three days. I discovered no one in the town ever complained to anyone about it. Soon I became the town's man to get it switched back on. Water was also a problem, along with communications. Internet was unheard of in this town!

I remember clearly what happened one day when we erected our tent in the main park in the town of Parramoss. I preached an evangelistic message majoring on living in sin. I was shocked when I made the call for those living in sin to come forward for prayer. Eight couples from our own church responded! The next few weeks we arranged eight weddings.

That was the last time I used the tent as I found out the meetings attracted more Christians than sinners! This is not what I wanted to happen.

Soon we would be in our new building – a place used earlier for prostitution! The owner was so shocked to hear we wanted to rent a house of sin for a church, he even brought the rent down in price. We had a large garden and were able to build a church to the glory of God. We soon grew to over two-hundred, had leaders set in place, and I taught them evangelism.

Two years later I felt restless again and knew it was time to seek God for new direction. We knew it was time to leave this church so for a short period of time, we returned to the Verbo Church in Jocotenango while we waited to hear from God.

Prior to moving to Parramoss, I had met a young pastor by the name of Fredy Lopez. He had just moved to Ciudad Vieja (The Old City) which was close by. Fredy had started up a new church and we attended some of his services. The "church building" was a garden with 4 poles stuck in the ground and a piece of plastic sheet for a roof. Our chairs were stumps of wood with a plank set across them.

It was pouring down with rain during the first service we attended. Believe me, when it rains in this country, it is monsoon weather! There we were worshipping the Lord with umbrellas, surrounded by chickens and dogs! One of the chickens actually jumped on the guy playing the guitar!

The people did not seem to worry. They sang so loudly I am sure the whole town heard them! Not having any walls had its downside. It was terribly cold and the wind swept straight through, along with the rain. We went home wet and cold, but very happy knowing this was the place we were supposed to be.

Soon we moved into a building which could hold about sixty people. It was not long before we had one hundred people inside! This is what happens when one evangelizes! We held services twice a week and it got very hot inside this windowless metal building. Again, it did not seem to bother the people.

It was in this building I realized I was the only one who got up and danced! They all looked at me and smiled, watching this lanky figure do the two-step Charismatic Samba! One night, as I was preaching. the Holy Spirit spoke to me and said, "Set them free!"

I started to preach on deliverance and soon there was a lot of screaming and crying coming from many people. As they got delivered, they began to dance and dance and dance… until they fell down with exhaustion. This was the moment I knew God was doing something big with these people.

One day I was invited to share in another small church. There were quite a few alcoholics present and, together with my Guatemalan team, I began to minister to them.

"Brother Jeff, brother Jeff come over here quickly!" shouted Juan, one of my team members. He was completely flustered.

At the time, I was praying for a lady and told them to wait.

"No! It can't wait, you have to come now!" shouted Juan.

"What's the problem?" I asked.

"The lady wants to be un-saved!" he said anxiously.

I thought I was not hearing him right in Spanish, so after calming him down, I asked him to speak slowly and tell me the problem again.

"The lady wants to be un-saved," he repeated. "I don't know what to do."

I had to turn my face away and chuckle to myself. Un-saved? Was there such a thing in the Bible?

I spoke with this lady. She had a cigarette in her mouth as she explained that she had accepted Jesus Christ as her Lord and Saviour the previous week. She was now finding it too hard to stop smoking, hence she wanted to be "un-saved!"

"O Lord you really do send the strangest people to me." I thought to myself.

I spent the next twenty minutes sharing with her that God had not given up on her and with time her smoking would stop. She happily accepted that and left the church with a big smile on her face, and the cigarette still dangling out of her mouth!

Our church in Ciudad Vieja was not growing as fast as I wanted it to. I began seeking the Lord as to why we were not winning more people to the Kingdom. A few days later, Christa and I visited a church in the main city called Casa de Dios (House of God). It had a membership of about twenty-two thousand. The pastor's name was Carlos Luna.

During the service a man shared about the miracle of his own life. He had been in an accident and for years was in a state of vegetation, not able to see, move his legs or arms. Pastor Carlos prayed over him and immediately he was able to see and walk again.

These testimonies excite me, as I too have seen some incredible miracles and healings when I have prayed for people.

Pastor Carlos Luna shared that God had given him a new vision and that soon he would have one of the largest churches in Guatemala. Since its inception, the Lord spoke saying the church was not born in the heart of a man, but of God and it would experience the manifestation of His presence.

When his congregation had reached about sixty people, the Holy Spirit was poured out on many of them which left them drunk in the Spirit, something they had never experienced, just as happened with the disciples on the day of Pentecost. Since then, the church has grown supernatural, as many hungry and thirsty people have come to the Lord for the touch of the Holy Spirit in their lives.

Soon they moved to a building which could house 5,000, but the church very quickly grew to over 26,000. Pastor Cash heard from God and implemented a model called "The Jesus Model" which is based on how Jesus discipled His twelve apostles.

This model is based on the biblical principle of being a blessing to each in a group person to achieve multiplication. It involves cell groups who evangelize, disciple, and send people out to start new cell groups. Casa de Dios has since moved into yet another new building which houses 12,000. In just a few short years they have grown to over 26,000 members and have over 5,000 cell groups.

Pastor Fredy and I attended some of their conferences to learn the new model and implement it in our church. Very soon we could not fit another person into our building. Our cell groups soon reached thirty and we soon realized we had to find another building.

Christa and I have always kept in touch with our supporters with newsletters and postcards. This is very important as they are our lifeline. It was not long before we found another piece of land and our supporters helped us purchase it and construct a new building to house about 500 members. I insisted our own church members also contribute towards the building. They are extremely poor by Western standards, but they gave generously, sometimes selling many of their private belongings. We are truly proud of them!

Chapter 18

The Dangers

Guatemala with all its beauty also has a dark side. Because of its great poverty and corruption at government level, many of the poor turn to crime to survive and the crime rate is high. Mafia drug cartels are forever at war with each other for control of their territories, and the murder rate is approximately twenty a day. Many of these gangs come from Mexico because the murder rate is even higher there!

Teenage gangs control the streets and receive protection money from the busses, taxis and businesses. If you do not pay, you end up dead. Each day the newspapers report yet another taxi or bus driver murdered and more corrupt police arrested. In the nineteen years we have been in Guatemala, they have had seven new Police Chiefs. Some of them are now behind bars. In a local canning factory near to us, the director of the factory and the Police Chief were arrested for canning drugs, disguised as soups, and sending them to Europe.

One day Christa was in our church when she heard a gunshot. She looked out of the window and was shocked to see one of our youth leaders had been murdered. One of the requirements of gang initiation ceremonies for new members is they must kill someone. Sadly, this young man was in the wrong place at the wrong time.

Whilst writing this book yet another member of our church has been murdered. Life is cheap in this country and many people get away with murder because the police cannot handle the volume of killings. As missionaries, we do not have time to be scared of what is going on, but we always ask our supporters for their prayers for protection.

Another day I was driving around the town of Antigua trying to find a parking space. I went around the block four times and eventually decided to park on a red line outside the shop I wanted to enter. As I got out of my car, the vehicle travelling behind me stopped suddenly. Five policemen pointed guns at my head. They roughly pushed me against my car and did a quick search.

"I only parked on a red line! Isn't this carrying things a bit too far?" I protested. "Okay, I'll pay the fine! I'll pay the fine!"

They were not amused. They informed me they were a special unit and insisted I was a suspected criminal on the FBI's most wanted criminals list. As a matter of fact. I was just below Bin Laden on their list!

I assured them I was British, but that did not seem to work. They told me the man they were looking for had a walking stick; he had had a back operation, and sported a scar over his left eye. Sadly so did I! When I asked to look at the picture of the man, they showed me a photocopy of a photocopy of a photocopy. The picture was so black it was unrecognizable.

By this time a big crowd had gathered and people were saying, "Isn't that Hermano Jeff the missionary?"

How embarrassed I felt! I was somewhat worried that if I made one wrong move they were ready to kill me. They were excited because they honestly thought they had caught the second most wanted man on the FBI list. I could just see them celebrating in the evening and telling their colleagues whom they had caught!

They took me to their offices and by this time the American Embassy Consulate had arrived. He was unsure what to do.

"Listen old chap," I said, "Can't you see I am British? I drink tea not coffee, so I am not American!"

A worried Christa arrived with my passport to prove I was British, but they thought my passport could be false. I telephoned the British Embassy and they advised me to ask them whether I was under arrest.

"No," they answered, "But it would be better if you stayed here."

So slowly, very slowly I said, "I am going home and taking my documents with me"

One of the police was a woman and she kept saying, "We are truly sorry."

So was I, and with that I slowly got into my car, started the engine and gave a little sickly wave to the American Embassy Consulate. He was still their twiddling his fingers! Driving home, I wondered if I would get a knock on my door or even have it kicked in.

By the way, if you go to the FBI wanted list website you will see the name Robert William Fisher. Now ask yourself, do I really look like him? Besides, I do not chew tobacco and am no longer super-fit!

I am glad I never used my army training to fight off the policemen in self-defense or maybe I would not be writing this book!

Sadly, since this episode I have gone down to sixth place as the most wanted!

Chapter 19

The Ministry

As an evangelist, my love is to see people brought into the kingdom. I have taught second generations in our church in Ciudad Vieja on how to evangelize and that is why our church ng at a fairly fast pace.

Each new convert attends a weekend encounter; one for men and one for women. This involves a time of inner healing, deliverance, and establishing a new identity in Jesus Christ as they are integrated into the River of God (Win, Consolidate, Disciple and Send out).

Twice a year we ran discipleship academy courses lasting eight months, culminating with a graduation ceremony in the church. A special prize was handed out to the student with the highest scores over the eight months. On these evenings the church overflowed with parents and friends who come to witness the graduation. This has opened new ways of winning new converts for the Lord. We have baptized more than 2,500 people over the years!

Visiting houses, prayers stations, campaigns, and film nights are all ways of winning people to the Kingdom of God, but our ministry goes much deeper than these excellent ways of evangelism. Because there is such poverty, we often get people coming to our house asking for financial help. Each case is different. We do not always help financially to avoid making the people dependent on the missionaries. What we do is give them advice on employment, etc.

Others are sick and need to visit doctors or buy medicines, and this is where we always help. We have a "Helps Fund" kept flowing by our supporter's contributions. Believe me when I say it empties very quickly! During our time in Guatemala, many lives have been saved through this fund.

One needs to be very flexible as a missionary and always ready to be called out 24/7. We serve as taxi drivers, ambulance drivers, dentists, doctors, carpenters, electricians, Godparents, best man, loan merchants (although never getting a cent back!), advisors and, of course, teachers and preachers. Christa is very involved in all areas of missions work, often doing twice as much as me!

Over the years we have seen many miracles and healings. One of the most amazing was a man raised from the dead. This man beat his wife and children and was always drunk. Can you imagine this man being laid in his coffin and then God speaking to our young pastor to go and raise him from the dead?

Well, that is exactly what happened. As he entered the house there were many people weeping over the dead man. He told them to leave the house and in faith laid his hands on the dead man. Seconds later the man rose out of his coffin. The people outside were stunned. They shrieked as they rushed into the house!

Why would God raise up a man who was not even a Christian? I believe the reason was to show the many people present that the Word is true.

> *"Heal the sick, raise the dead, cure those with leprosy, and cast out demons. Give as freely as you have received!" Matthew 10:8.*

Up and until this time eighteen people who saw this miracle had been worshipping the idol called Mashimon. All eighteen received Christ as their Lord and Savior and became members of our church!

Despite all the evil, we continue to pray for the sick and see many healings. One night as I was about to preach in the church, I felt led to say God wanted to heal people with poor eyesight. Seven women came forward and all received instant healing. On another occasion, a man in his last days with cancer was instantly healed when I laid my hands on him.

Men, women, and children with all forms of sickness have been healed, and on many occasions we have cast demons out of people. We know this is not us, but the Holy Spirit who lives within. It is He who gets all the glory; we are only his willing tools.

> *"Don't you realize that your body is the temple of the Holy Spirit, who lives in you and was given to you by God? You do not belong to yourself"* 1 Corinthians 6:19.

One day I was called to someone's home and the family told me they had ghosts in their house.

"What made them believe that?" I asked.

What they told me was quite shocking! Each night after they went to bed, they heard noises in the kitchen and banging on the windows. They were too scared to investigate. Every morning when they went into the kitchen, they found their table laid for breakfast. knives, forks and spoons, along with plates, would be laid out on the table!

As I entered the house with a friend, I could feel the presence of evil spirits. My friend and I took charge of the problem and cast out the demons causing these things to happen. The next day we visited the family and they told us with smiling faces that the manifestations had stopped. Weeks later we learned that the houses in that area were built on an old graveyard.

In 2010 one of the many volcanoes exploded and people close by were killed by the hot lava which flowed rapidly down the volcano. Volcanic ash covered the majority of Guatemala City up to four-inches thick. The main airport had to be closed down for a number of days.

Two weeks later Hurricane Agatha struck Guatemala, and especially our town of Ciudad Vieja. A river half-way up the volcano Agua near us overflowed its banks, sending boulders as big as houses and a tide of mud and water in its wake. People in our town fled their houses and we put them up in our church building.

Sadly, one of our families did not get out of their house quickly enough and was carried away with the mud. Their house became rubble. We found a mother and her grandchild from our church buried in the mud three days later. The next day we held the funeral and both mother and grandchild were placed in the same grave. Over the next two days, there were another fourteen funerals in our town.

Our Globe Mission organization and our church in Germany made an emergency donation raised within 24 hours. With this we were able to buy food, towels, shoes, and clothes for families who had lost everything. As more people answered our appeal for funds, we were able to help more families.

Each year we have a short-term mission project called "People Building People," Those who come help build a house in five days. They also assist with the running of a medical and dental campaign and children's bible school.

Many of these good people arrived to help rebuild some of the local's houses that were destroyed. Much of the funds received were put to this use. What better way is there to share the love of Jesus. We thank the directors of the mission, John and Sue Gadsby, for their service to the people. They have helped to build 11 houses as I write this book.

Chapter 20

Health

Although Guatemala is a third world country, it does have some top-rated private hospitals, unlike the national hospitals which are not at all very nice. On occasions I have visited patients in tional hospitals and was shocked with the conditions I saw.

Many patients are left on trolleys in the passage-ways as there are no beds. The rooms are packed bed to bed, and in some instances patients are handcuffed to the railings. These are the gang members who were injured with gunshot wounds. I talked with some of them and was surprised to find they had been waiting over two months for an operation just to remove a bullet! Patients had their food stolen by other patients, whilst others had their clothes stolen.

Many people on kidney dialysis machines die due to the fact they do not have enough machines or medicines. People who need an operation have to first buy all the necessary medicines needed, and then wait up to 3 months for their operation! All I could do was share the Gospel with these people.

In our previous church, we had four ex-gang members who were saved. One of these was an ex-murderer and rapist who, after serving his sentence, got wonderfully saved. God does not give up on these gangs. Jesus came for this purpose.

> *"Then he added, "Now go and learn the meaning of this Scripture: 'I want you to show mercy, not offer sacrifices.' For I have come to call not those who think they are righteous, but those who know they are sinners" Matthew 9:13.*

The people we work with are very poor and generally have a short lifespan, on average of fifty-five years. This is because of the conditions they live in and their poor diet. Many have sugar diabetes. I'm not surprised because when we get invited for a cup of coffee, I think there is more sugar in the coffee than coffee!

Although we help many of these people, we can only do so much. Their roofs leak, beds get wet, and the mud floors affect the children, who often get very ill. We have attended many funerals as a result.

I thank God it is compulsory for missionaries to have health insurance. One day whilst at a children's birthday party, I slipped and something went click in my back. I was in a lot of pain, but managed to last the time while attempting to put on a brave smile.

A few days later I was walking in Antigua and tripped over the cobblestones. Something clicked in my back again. The town of Antigua is all cobblestones, and many times the stones come loose. I was in tremendous pain, but somehow managed to crawl to my car and drive home in agony. After some medicine, the pain subsided for a while.

During the coming weeks, we flew to Germany and then decided to fly to England to show our daughter, Antonia, my country. Whilst in London, I found it even harder to walk and was in tremendous pain. On returning to Germany, I took pain killers but they did not seem to help. We then flew back to Guatemala and my conditioned worsened. I finally ended up in a private hospital in Guatemala City.

Over the next twelve years, I endured thirteen major operations on my lower spine. Somehow, between each of these operations, I continued my ministry, evangelizing daily and preaching in church on Sundays and Thursdays. Strangely, each time I got up in the pulpit the pain disappeared, but came back with a vengeance afterwards. Miracles and healings still continued from my ministry, but not for my own back.

Eventually in 2011, Christa and I visited the church Casa de Dios in the city hoping that pastor Cash Luna could pray for me. Unfortunately, he was in Spain but our Guatemalan pastor friend, Rodolfo Mendoza, prayed over me and I received instant healing! O Hallelujah, what joy I had! My back had two solid bars with four screws, making it impossible to bend, but bend I did! Hallelujah, even with the bars in my back!

A couple of weeks later, Pastor Rodolfo telephoned me early one Sunday morning.

"Jeff, you must come down to our church at twelve a-clock," He said excitedly, "We are doing a live-televised "Day of Miracles" program over Central America.

"Sorry, my friend, but I am preaching twice today in our church," I responded.

"You have to come, Jeff!" he shouted down the telephone.

"Oh man," I replied, "I will try and make it there."

I preached a shortened message that morning, excused myself to the Lord and the congregation, and drove the fastest I had ever driven to Guatemala City/ A slightly pale-faced Christa never uttered a word!

Pastor Rodolfo was waiting for me. 5,000 people were in the church and cameras were everywhere. Two doctors quickly examined me and looked at the x-rays before allowing me on the platform. One of the doctors spoke clearly and confirmed that it would be impossible for me to bend with these types of rods in my back, but bend I did!

They were shocked but overjoyed, and the audience went wild with delight. One doctor on the stage hugged me and shook his head with disbelief.

"I want to tell you these bars are impossible to bend," he said loudly as he looked at the pictures of my back. "Impossible!" he repeated joyfully.

"There is more metal in this x-ray than in my car!" Pastor Cash Luna joked.

Everyone was clapping and cheering as we ran to the car and rushed home. We arrived back just in time for the afternoon service in our church. It was certainly an exhausting day, but a happy one indeed.

But tragically, my joy came to an end and I was truly shattered when the pain came back a year later! I was broken in my spirit and completely devastated. I could not believe this was happening to me. How could God allow this to happen to me when I had faithfully served Him all these years?

"Lord, why?" I cried. "Why have you allowed this to happen? You sent Christa and me to Guatemala to do your Kingdom work, and now this!"

I started to have doubts about healing. After a day or two of having a pity-party, I decided I would not remain in this condition and so I continued to pray for the sick, I saw healings and even miracles, but still agonized with the pain in my back. God was not giving any answer to my prayers about my condition.

Once more I was wheeled into the operating theatre of one of Guatemala's finest hospitals. I was soon to find out what was going on in the spiritual world.

I woke up in the intensive care ward to the sight of demons flying about and people screaming. The stench was overpowering and I began to vomit.

"Lord, Lord, I am so weak, take these away!" I screamed as the nurses came rushing in to find out what was going on!

God brought peace to my room. Was I hallucinating? No, I saw hell in all its fury. I saw thousands of demons, fire, and people screaming. It was so evil, I cannot even begin to describe it today.

The next night still in intensive care, I had a bad dream. I dreamed I was in some small town, but I am not certain what country it was. The town was having a parade and whipping up support to join their movement. A brass band was playing and people were handing out leaflets. The stench was nauseating; it was something like old cigarettes and beer! I knew that smell from my military days of old before I became a Christian.

I was amazed at my involvement in this dream. I was actually sabotaging everything ahead of the parade, ripping down posters and flags, pushing my way forward, and keeping out of the way of the police who were looking for me. But soon they caught me and I was brought before the leaders of this movement. Rather than punish me, they actually offered me a high position in their movement. Something in my spirit told me what they were doing was wrong, and I woke up in a sweat, still aware of the nauseating smell.

A few days later, with tears in my eyes, I pleaded with my doctor to move me out of the intensive care unit back into my room, but even there the nauseating smell persisted. Eventually I pleaded with him to allow me to go home.

Hospitals are places where many people die and the spirit of death looms over them. Many of the people who die there are not Christians so you can imagine the spiritual atmosphere in these places. Back at home I had an abnormal high sense of smell which caused me constant nausea. I could not eat anything for over ten days.

All I had heard from the Lord at this stage was to write a book on my experience of seeing hell.

I was soon to have an answer to my many "whys?"

Chapter 21

Feeling Sorry

As I lay in bed, I listened to a preaching tape some friends from the USA had sent me. I knew within the first ten minutes the message was for me.

Part of the message was about a pastor who went to a meeting of a well-known British evangelist by the name of Smith-Wigglesworth. This pastor watched as two men carried an elderly and very frail lady onto the platform. She was wheezing and was very ill with cancer.

"Let her go!" Smith-Wigglesworth cried out. She fell flat on her face.

"Pick her up!" he said; then "Let her go!"

"Pastor, this woman will die if we let her go," exclaimed his worried workers.

Undeterred, Wigglesworth cried out, "Let her go!"

Again, she fell flat on her face.

"Pick her up!" commanded Wigglesworth.

A man in the audience shouted out, "Smith-Wigglesworth, you are a monster! Stop it!"

Wigglesworth calmly turned to the gentleman. "Sir," he said, "you mind your own business. and I will mind mine. Now sit down!"

"Let her go!" he continued.

With that command, she began to fall again, but this time she put her own foot out to stop her fall. Suddenly a large cancer fell from her body onto the platform – she was completely healed.

> *"Heal the sick, raise the dead, cure those with leprosy, and cast out demons. Give as freely as you have received!"* Matthew 10:8.

This pastor who had watched Smith-Wigglesworth was so excited at what he saw, on the following Sunday he held a healing service. He was fired up and wanted to see all these things happen in his church. Healings began to happen.

Then a man in a wheelchair was brought forward. Still fired up, the pastor commanded the man to be pulled up out of the chair.

"Let him go!" he shouted.

The man fell flat on his face. People gasped in horror. The young pastor ran to the man, apologizing and comforting him. What was this pastor's error? He was moving on the faith of Smith-Wigglesworth and not his own! Would the man in the wheelchair have been healed had the pastor continued to allow to him to fall, not only three times, but maybe ten times? That pastor's faith was no longer strong after seeing the man fall.

I learnt something that day. We can only move in our own faith, not in the faith of others.

> *"Faith is the confidence that what we hope for will actually happen; it gives us assurance about things we cannot see"* Hebrews 11:1.

I realized I had stated many, many times to people that I had great faith to see healings and miracles in their bodies, but not in my own! There is power in what one speaks, and I was speaking negative words.

> *"For the word of God is alive and powerful. It is sharper than the sharpest two-edged sword, cutting between soul and spirit,*

between joint and marrow. It exposes our innermost thoughts and desires" Hebrews 4:12.

The dream I had came back to me, like a knife stabbing me in my back. God does not want me to "follow the band" – i.e. following the majority of Christians today who are not walking in mighty signs and wonders, preaching a gospel so weak that more people leaving the Church than entering it. In my dream I was sabotaging the efforts of lukewarm Christians that blend in and run along with the world. In real life I was not "walking the talk." In reality I was preaching the whole Bible but not living it!

Yes, our church here in Guatemala had grown to over five hundred, but now I was concerned how many true Christians we had inside it? In ten years over two thousand five hundred people had passed through our church, and yet we now have only had five hundred! What happened to the two thousand? I was shocked, that some of them could go to that place called Hell for eternity.

You see, getting someone to say, "I believe that Jesus died on the cross for my sins," does not bring brokenness. We need to ensure the person knows there is the wrath of Hell to come and he must flee from it. There is no genuine repentance without it.

Ask yourselves today whether you have truly been convicted of your sin. Were you truly broken and were you told about the wrath of Hell and that you needed to repent? Or were you sold a "Love, Joy, and Peace Gospel?" Take a few minutes and be truthful with yourself.

As I finished listening to the taped message, my old Guatemalan friend, Marco Estrada, came in to see me. We had not seen each other for over a year and now he had heard about my operation.

Here I was lying in bed, feeling sorry for myself. Marco Estrada is one remarkable man of God. He has no money, and yet his ministry stretches out right across Guatemala in six-hundred villages where he works with poor farmers, elderly pastors, and many others teaching them how to stay healthy with natural food. Of course, the most important part of his ministry is the Gospel. (If you wish to have more information, contact me).

I shared with Marco about what had happened and he smiled broadly as he opened his Bible at James 5:16.

> *"Confess your sins to each other and pray for each other so that you may be healed. The earnest prayer of a righteous person has great power and produces wonderful results."*

Immediately I confessed my lack of faith to Marco. I felt genuine peace come across me at that moment as if a large burden had been lifted from me.

I can still bend my back, which in itself is a miracle. Every time I preach the Word, any pain that I had disappears. My faith has returned one-hundred percent and I know God will again bring complete healing to me.

Say what you like, I continue to trust in my Redeemer. I do not always understand God's ways, but I do know that I trust Him with all my heart and with my life.

Healing is for everyone, including me.

Chapter 22

Preach the Truth

Now my next step was to change completely how I would evangelize in the future. I do not want to see our church filled with sheep and goats.

> *"The people of all nations will be brought before him, and he will separate them, as shepherds separate their sheep from their goats"* Matthew 25:32.

Jesus is going to send the goats to Hell. I am sure He will be weeping for them, but then it will be too late. Hell is for eternity. I saw it, but cannot even begin to describe that evil place.

In my home country of Great Britain there are many fields where one can see sheep and goats grazing together. They are hard to tell apart from afar. This I believe is the same in many of our churches across the world. People look like Christians, they even sing those beautiful songs, and some of them might even be in the choirs, or even pastors. It is time to study ourselves to see if we are approved.

> *"Work hard so you can present yourself to God and receive his approval. Be a good worker, one who does not need to be ashamed and **who correctly explains the word of truth***"* 2 Timothy 2:15.

So, the question again is: Have we been correctly explaining the Word truthfully? Well, I know I have not. But now, after being allowed to see Hell and not even being able to explain what I saw because of the evil, I intend to do a one-hundred percent turn around on preaching the Gospel.

Listen to these words from Charles Spurgeon:

> *"Lower the Law, and you dim the light by which man perceives his guilt. This is a very serious loss to the sinner, rather than a gain; for it lessens the likelihood of his conviction and conversion.... I say that you have deprived the gospel of its most powerful weapon when you have set aside the Law. You have taken away from it the schoolmaster that is to bring men to Christ… they will never accept grace till they tremble before a just and holy Law. Therefore the Law serves a most necessary and blessed purpose and it must not be removed from its place.*

When the sinner sees the awful consequences of breaking the Law of Almighty God, and there is no way he can escape the certainty of judgment, he will then see his need to run to Jesus Christ – the only One who can save him.

We must preach future punishment by the Law, and then the sinners will come to Christ solely to flee from "the wrath of Hell that is to come." Everyone, but everyone will die.

> *"Just as people are destined to die once, and after that to face judgment"* Hebrews 9:27.

Even though my back is not yet completely healed, God has given me an even **greater passion** than ever to share the true Gospel with as many people as is possible. Jesus Christ is coming very soon and I do not wish to see even one person going to Hell,

Sadly, at this very moment there are about one-hundred-fifty thousand people A DAY going right there… for ETERNITY. Maybe they were never truly convicted by the Gospel we shared with them. I am sure you know of many who have left your church and gone back into the world. Go after them, I beg of you! Go after them and share the true Gospel, not a "Greasy-Grace Gospel."

An important part of ministry is always seeking the Lord to see if He has anything new for us to do for His Kingdom. In the world there are multitudes of people who are lost, and God desires us to help them through the power of the Holy Spirit.

Over the past years, I have had three prophecies that our ministry in Guatemala will not end, and that I will be invited to preach in many countries. Sure enough, the invitations have started to pour in. This is, of course, very exciting, but at the same time I know I need to hear clearly from the Lord when and where to go. Just as Moses heard God say:

"My presence shall go with you and I will give you rest"
Exodus 33:14.

I too need to hear the Father speak to me. for without His presence I cannot carry His Word with His power.

Chapter 23

India

For three years I built a relationship with Pastor Sonu Singh and his wife, Pinky, in Amroha which is in Northern India In September of 2012, I felt it was time to pay them a visit. My roots started in India and I always had a desire to visit this country. Both my parents lived in India during the time of the British Empire when I was just a twinkle in my father's eyes!

After a very comfortable flight with British Airways direct to New Delhi, I at long last met Sonu & Pinky in the flesh. We had often communicated by video phone over the past three years, but this was quite emotional. We had a three-hour drive in front of us and there was no way I was going to sleep! The drivers in India are crazy and never stop blowing their horns! Many times I thought I was going to meet my Maker sooner than expected.

I was shown around their humble rented home and was soon treated to one of the delights of Pinky's home – made curries. Believe me, it was delicious

They now have eighteen pastors in their ministry and have established over fifty house-churches, but their vision is to set up many more! Two donated motorbikes help them get around to the various locations where they had started churches. Some of these churches are over three hours away in the northern jungle.

That evening they took me to meet Sonu's parents, who also live in humble circumstances. As the sun went down – but not the temperature – I watched some of monkeys swing from tree to tree, Yes, this was definitely different from Guatemala.

I rested well the first night and the following morning needed to use the lavatory. To my surprise, it was just a hole in the ground. That not being bad enough, I looked around for toilet paper but there was none to be found! I will not tell you how I dealt with this problem! Showering was even more interesting and consisted of throwing a basin of water over oneself. At least it was cooling as the temperatures inside and outside the house must have been over forty centigrade!

Dressed and ready, I joined them for breakfast. We all sat cross-legged on a couple of large double-beds pushed together. By this time, I was already sweating profusely. It felt as if I had never dried myself after having my "shower."

Later in the morning, we left for an evangelistic outreach. Sonu and his team had erected a large tent, but we found out later it could not even accommodate half the people who came! Over four thousand attended, some people coming from as far away as five hundred kilometers! Word surely gets around fast when a stranger is in town!

After a good hour of worship played just with bongos and a small keyboard (no trouble with this worship team!), the leaders came onto the platform and presented me with floral garlands as a sign of respect. I was really touched and tears began to openly flow down my face. Then came my introduction and I shared the Gospel.

Afterward, hundreds of Hindus received Christ as their Lord and Savior, rejecting the thousands of other gods they used to worship. The Lord then followed the Word with many miracles and healings. The deaf were hearing again, many of them! The lame were walking, many of them! Other sicknesses were healed, and demons were cast out.

I was sweating profusely as I prayed for these wonderful people. Even though there were people fanning me, I am sure I must have lost a few pounds on my first day.

The meeting ended after about six hours. We visited a few houses, where we continued to pray for many more people. The following day, being Sunday, I was woken up quite early and told some people had come to the house expecting me to pray for them!

Sonu was looking tired but I felt quite well, especially after the breakfast of Curry and Parathas. One thing I was truly happy was that Pinky knew I drank lots of tea, so my cup was also kept well filled.

At 11.00 am we left to visit the Jungle village of Madhupri, a three-hour drive away. Sonu told me about the tigers, elephants, monkeys, snakes, and other animals in the jungle and I was a little bit apprehensive as to what to expect. But God was in charge, so I placed that at the back of my mind as we went down narrow dirt roads with big holes in them.

There were seven hundred people in this Hindu village and Sonu and his team had brought them to the Lord – A whole village saved! They also built a church, donated by one of the women in the village after she got saved, but it still needed a roof. With the help of God, I was able to give them the necessary funds for the roof. Next to the church building, Sonu had fitted a water pump for the villagers. What a blessing for the people.

The next day we all woke up feeling tired, but happy with what the Lord was doing among us. After a time of prayer and refreshing and some breakfast, Sonu and Pinky took me on a rickshaw through the town to buy some gifts for my family. How we never got killed on that rickshaw is beyond me!

Once more the hot weather took its toll on me and I was glad to sit in a shop where they had electric fans. A quick fizzy drink brought relief to me as Pinky chose a typical dress for Christa and my daughter, Antonia, as well as gifts for Edwin and my grandson, Jeffrey.

After a snack lunch and some rest, Sonu informed me we would be visiting a few families who had invited us to come and pray for them. Then we were to return to our first venue where quite a few people had gathered for a prayer meeting.

At the first house, I was offered hot goats milk which I thoroughly enjoyed, and then plenty of water and tea. At each house we visited we had the same, plus cake and biscuits. I enjoyed praying for the families and their homes. A big surprise was to follow!

We expected about twenty or thirty people to attend the prayer meeting, but over one thousand arrived! I was shocked. They hastily erected a high platform with a sound system and put a worship group together. Later I had heard that some people had come from as far away as three-hundred miles. Word indeed traveled fast.

The National had paper published my picture with the headline: "Preacher comes to share about the True God." Obviously many people read this. Others came because they heard about the many miracles that had taken place. Everyone was talking about this God who was using men to heal them of their sicknesses and that certainly got them interested.

We removed our shoes and put with the many hundreds of other pairs. (It's a wonder people find their shoes later). We walked to the platform with people attempting to touch us. I watched as people climbed high walls and houses to get a glimpse of what was going on!

Little did I know "quiet prayer meeting" was going to go on for over ten hours and leave me with only an hour or two to get ready for my flight back to Germany! I was glad for the big electric fan blowing into my face during the worship, plus the two people at the back fanning me with their home-made fans, what a luxury!

As the worship continued, so did the manifestation of many demons and soon we were down among the people casting out these evil demons and bring healing and many miracles to them all. Again, many people received Christ as their Lord and Savior.

After what seemed like hours, two men heaved me bodily onto the platform again to rest a bit. I was glad of this and soon cold water was brought to quench my thirst and cool my profusely sweating body.

The people didn't want me to take a break and jumped on the platform to get prayed for. After a while there were so many on the platform, for my own safety I was literally carried off by two "minders" and taken to Sonu's mother's house. I was placed in a chair, and what came next was just ecstasy! They massaged my legs and feet, while one other woman massaged my neck – heaven!

Someone said, "The holy man is in the house!" and soon people clambered over the twelve-foot high wall, even though the meeting was still going on.

As tired as I was, I could not stop praying for these beautiful people who had seen God perform so many miracles. One by one they were brought to me, and one by one they were ALL healed! At the same time at the meeting, Sonu and his team were seeing hundreds of miracles and healings.

Such simple faith! I remember Jesus said, "Only Believe." Nothing more, nothing less. Yet we in the West make things so difficult for ourselves.

I asked why people touched my feet after I prayed for them and heard this was a sign of respect. I felt so humbled to be used by God in India. With my body still being fanned and having drunk what felt like the whole village well, I continued to pray and pray having no idea what time it was, except that it is was night time.

My greatest joy was asking the Hindu people if they wished to receive Christ as their Lord and Savior and renounce their gods. And then to see the joy on their faces as they were set free.

Whole families came forward for prayer and told me through Pinky, interpreting as best she could, that each night they were disturbed by demons. I was able to cast these demons out and tell them they were new creations in Christ and they would now sleep in peace. I heard later from pastor Sonu that these families indeed had no more problems with demons.

Meanwhile back at the meeting, Sonu had to call the police to control the crowds. We had not expected so many people, otherwise, he would have arranged police security.

Soon Sonu and the team came back to the house and I was again escorted by men, one each side of me and one in front. I felt like one of those superstars you see on TV surrounded by bodyguards! But this time it was to get me to the car as there were so many people waiting outside the house.

Soon we were on our way back to the ministry house. I looked at my watch – we had been ministering for over ten hours forty-five minutes! At the house, Pinky was preparing dinner. I quietly declined and fell into bed hoping to sleep, but I couldn't. I just kept thanking God for all that had happened that day and every day. Then the electricity went off again and, of course, the fans. Sonu and team somehow got some sort of cooling system going, but by then it was time to get up! I had been in bed just over two hours, exhausted but happy.

Pinky made me my usual cup of hot tea and then we went into the prayer room.

"Two men have been waiting outside all night for prayer," Sonu told me.

I prayed for them. Then I prayed for the team and I told them they were such a blessing. I knew by this time God had spoken clearly to me that this was to be a new ministry for both Christa and me. But there was a sinister reason why God had spoken to me. This would be cleared up later.

We drove the three-hour trip to the airport and I had to hold back my tears as I said goodbye to Sonu and Pinky and some of the team. I knew this was not the final goodbye and that soon I would return.

There is a great need for the Gospel to be shared in Northern India, an area that has hardly been evangelized. The harvest is truly ripe! I was touched to find out there were many days when they would all go without food because of lack of funds. Later I found this out one of the biggest problems of Sonu obtaining help is the lack of trust in the Western world. It is well known there are many false pastors on the social networks, like Facebook and elsewhere, who have false ministries just to obtain money from the Western world.

Again, at this time I did not know that Sonu was also obtaining money under false pretenses!

Sonu and Pinky had "adopted" both Christa and myself as their Mum and Dad, and as such have given us full authority to speak into their lives and help their ministry, which we have been doing over the past few years. Some people who had visited their ministry put negative remarks on the Web and I believed at the time they had been sent by the devil. Later on, I was to find out it was the truth!

After my return to Germany (I had traveled from Germany to India), I met with our Mission Director, Brad Thurston, and his co-workers and shared with them about my trip to India. Without exception, they were all thrilled and gave me their support for our future work in India.

Christa and I are convinced God Himself opened a door for us to work in North India, together with a local pastor and his team. We are to:

"Preach the gospel to the poor, to heal the brokenhearted, to proclaim liberty to the captives and recovery of sight to the blind, to set at liberty those who are oppressed and to proclaim the acceptable year of the Lord" Luke 4:18-19.

I know God wants me to go again, so I ask for your prayers for a miracle for my back.

Chapter 24

Second Mission to India

My second mission trip to Northern India to visit the ministry of Pastor Sonu Singh took place from 16 to 24 November 2012, and this time I was accompanied by Christa. After a trip via Abu Dhabi to New Delhi, we were met by Pastor Sonu and his wife Pinky. We had a further three-hour trip to the town of Amroha in the district of Utter Pradesh. This was not such a hair-raising experience as my first visit because and there was less traffic about when we arrived at 3 am.

As nothing was arranged for the first day, we took a Rickshaw ride into town for Christa to purchase some Indian clothes. I must admit, all of them were so beautiful it was difficult to choose which was best for her. But I knew that if I didn't get her out of the shop, she would probably buy the whole stock!

That evening we visited the parents of Pastor Sonu. What a joy it was to meet them the second time. After many cups of Indian Chai tea (delicious), we collapsed into our beds truly worn out.

When I had previously come in August, temperatures reached 40 centigrade. The electricity often failed, and with it the ventilation seemed to fail at night time too, which left me soaking in sweat. This time it was a pleasant 27 Centigrade. Again, bathing was throwing cold water over oneself. In the morning before the sun rose it was quite cold! Using the toilet was a new experience for Christa but she soon got used to the ceramic hole in the ground!

The next day after a scrambled egg sandwich breakfast and lots of Chai tea, we left for our first crusade in the town of Bazpur, a journey of about three-hours. The massive tent had already been set up the day before by Pastor Daniel Singh – a cousin of Sonu Singh. When we arrived, there was a massive police presence as some radical Hindus did not want us in their town! After introductions and flowers were hung around our necks, some of the town officials spoke.

I was surprised to be told I only had two minutes to speak! Expecting a riot, Pastor Sonu told me the town officials had asked us to leave. We would be permitted to come back the next day and hold our crusade.

As Christa and I were literally hassled off the platform, people pushed forward so I could lay my hands on them. Again, almost like some pop-star, we were pushed into the waiting car and driven off at top speed. Later I had heard that the wife of Pastor Daniel wielded a big stick, saying if any of the extremists Hindus wanted to lay their hands on any of us, they would have to pass by her first! Definitely a David in front of a giant!

The following day we came back to Bazpur, and again there was a heavy presence of police at the tent. This time I was allowed to share the Gospel and soon we were praying for the sick. But once again, after only fifteen minutes of praying, I was pulled away and shoved into the waiting car. The police had decided to leave and Pastor Sonu felt it was best to leave as well for our own safety.

This town has never heard of the name of Jesus Christ and we were apparently the first Europeans to enter it. I have since heard many miracles took place as we prayed and now the town officials want us to return in the future. We truly believe God had opened the door to these people and soon many will be saved and house churches established.

The next day was a rest day, but we really did not get any rest. We visited some families and ended up praying for many people.

Two crusades were scheduled for the following two days in the town on Kalali and the team had already set up the tent with sound equipment and a worship team. This was to be the cream on the cake, so to speak, as over two-thousand people received Christ as their Lord and Savior.

Miracles and healings took place as we ministered. I was deeply impacted to see five deaf people able to hear again. The looks on their faces said it all. One young boy who was dumb, said his first word: "HALLELUJAH!"

Christa was kept very busy praying as we gave every one of the large crowd personal prayer. On each of the days, we must have spent at least four hours praying for these people.

On our last day, we went to visit a family in another town, and many people turned out to look at us. The television people had interviewed us as well as the local papers and each day an article appeared in their newspaper. Try staying humble when so many people want to shake your hand as though you were some holy guru. But I am glad the Lord did keep us humble!

It was good we went to this village as I heard from Pastor Sonu that many Hindus received healing to their bodies and they want us to come back and hold a crusade.

You may be asking, what happens to all these people who have received Jesus Christ into their lives? They are all followed up. Pastor Sonu started a House Church in each town and they receive discipleship from members of his team. Soon this House Church would start other House Churches.

I asked Pastor Sonu if he had any idea how many people received Christ during his time of ministry and he humbly replied, "Maybe over 16,000 souls for Christ."

With CPM (Church Planting Movement) one cannot keep up with numbers of House Churches, and it has proved very effective in other parts of India, as well as around the world.

With House Churches, there are fewer expenses and no need to build church buildings or pay pastors. However, Pastor Sonu is the founder of *Salvation for Asia Ministries* and has many projects needing to be fulfilled for the ministry to run effectively. He is presently housed in a rented home and the owners are not very happy with so many visitors and the loud prayer meetings he holds daily. They need their own ministry house.

They also have to rent taxis each time people visit them, or when they have a big outreach in another town. There is therefore a need for a microbus and motorbikes.

Pastor Sonu seemed reluctant to give me a list of projects, but I insisted that people needed and wanted to know if they are to help him. One of these was for a generator as they like to show the Jesus film in villages where there is no electricity. Even when there is electricity, many times they have blackouts.

Chapter 25

Bad News

A couple of months after being in India, I received an email to say Sonu had a motor-bicycle accident and had hit a truck. In the email, Pinky explained he urgently needed an operation on 1, but they would not operate until a payment of $10,000 was received.

I found it strange they would let a patient die and I sensed in my spirit that something was not ringing true. Firstly, I knew Pinky could only speak a little English, and yet the email was written in almost perfect English. Secondly, I telephoned Pinky and found her voice different to the Pinky I knew. I emailed Pinky and asked her to send me a photograph of Sonu in the hospital. At first she said it was not allowed, but after insisting on a photograph, I eventually received one via email.

The picture I received made me burst out with laughter! There was Sonu with a bandage around his head, right arm, and left leg, but he was wearing dirty short pants and t-shirt. Firstly, a child could have done better bandaging than what I saw, and secondly, what was he doing wearing those dirty clothes after such an operation? I also noticed the bed he was in looked very much like the bed I slept in whilst I was in India. Even the pillow looked familiar! The denials kept coming!

"They allow double beds in the hospital and you have to bring your own pillows" wrote Pinky.

In the end, I knew who was writing the emails to me. Eventually he admitted that he had lied to get money from people. Later I found out he had fraudulently obtained more than $80,000 from different people, including myself.

I told Sonu that as I was his spiritual father, he needed to stand down from ministry for at least one year, and also pay back the money he had stolen from people. I was willing to go out again to see him and minister to him.

He refused. All pastors in India were stealing money and lying, he told me, so he found nothing wrong in doing the same!

I led him to the Bible where God spoke about liars and thieves not entering heaven. This did not seem to bother him and he said he would continue to steal and lie. I was devastated and could not believe he had spoken those words to me.

For the next few months, I warned as many people as possible about Sonu and also had to apologize to many of my friends who had given money to him. I felt my whole ministry was at stake and I took three months rest to recover from being taken in by this liar. My friends understood and told me they still trusted me.

I sought God for an answer as to why he opened this door for me to go to India, and especially to Sonu. Soon I was to get an answer from the Lord and I was quite surprised.

One of the pastors who had attended two of Sonu's meetings contacted me when he heard what Sonu had been doing. Pastor Trilok had his own ministry in Ghaziabad just outside New Delhi. He had been invited by Sonu, along with other pastors, to the meetings whilst I had been there. He was shocked to hear about Sonu's evil ways and had contacted me to apologize on behalf of pastors. He emphasized they were not all like Sonu. I stayed in contact with Pastor Trilok for over one year and he never once asked me for one single cent.

The Lord had sent me to India to pull this pastor away from Sonu, whilst at the same time to expose the ministry of Sonu to district pastors. They have since struck him off of their pastoral list. At the time of writing this book, it has been found that he was also having affairs with other women. I continue to pray that Sonu that one day he will come back to the Lord and confess his evil ways.

My hope and prayer is that pastor Sonu will come to understand that no matter how much ministry he is doing, it will not counteract the sin of stealing. I do believe God can do a miracle in Sonu. The work he does caring after the sick and opening up new house groups is a wonderful ministry.

Chapter 26

The Untouchables

After one year, I went back to India to visit Pastor Trilok and I loved the ministry he is doing with "The Untouchables." This man is working with street-children, the ones no one wants to ˌthing to do with. These people are called "The Untouchables."

More than 160 million people in India are considered "Untouchable" – people tainted by their birth into a caste system that deems them impure, and less than human.

Human rights abuses against these people, known as Dalits, are legion. A random sampling of headlines in mainstream Indian newspapers tells their story: "Dalit boy beaten to death for plucking flowers"; "Dalit tortured by cops for three days"; "Dalit 'witch' paraded naked in Bihar"; "Dalit killed in lock-up at Kurnool"; "Seven Dalits burnt alive in caste clash"; "Five Dalits lynched in Haryana"; "Dalit woman gang-raped, paraded naked"; "Police egged on mob to lynch Dalits".

India's Untouchables are relegated to the lowest jobs. They live in constant fear of being publicly humiliated, paraded naked, beaten, and raped with impunity by upper-caste Hindus seeking to keep them in their place. Merely walking through an upper-caste neighborhood, drinking from the same wells, attending the same temples, wearing shoes in the presence of an upper caste, or drinking from the same cups in tea stalls are life-threatening offences.

Statistics compiled by India's National Crime Records Bureau indicate that in the year 2000, the last year for which figures are available, 25,455 crimes were committed against Dalits. Every hour two Dalits are assaulted; every day three Dalit women are raped, two Dalits are murdered, and two Dalit homes are torched.

Despite the fact that untouchability was officially banned when India adopted its constitution in 1950, discrimination against Dalits remained pervasive. So much so that in 1989 the government passed legislation known as The Prevention of Atrocities Act.

The Act specifically made it illegal to parade people naked through the streets, force them to eat feces, take away their land, foul their water, interfere with their right to vote, and burn down their homes. Since then, the violence has escalated. This is largely a result of the emergence of a grassroots human rights movement among Dalits to demand their rights and resist the dictates of untouchability.

Pastor Trilok and his family built their first church a few years ago, right in the middle of these people, and have been winning them to the Lord. It has not been an easy job and he has been threatened many times.

I visited Trilok and his family on two occasions and not once did he ask me for any money. In fact, his family fed me and gave me gifts. What a change it was for me to see his honesty, and what a joy to preach to these beautiful people. On two occasions I visited his wife's ministry. She runs the children's Bible school. As I entered the church, the children sang a song to me and I could not hold back my tears.

I have since put Trilok in touch with a Christian American organization who were so impressed with his ministry they invested in Trilok, who can now speak very good English. He has even flown to Malaysia for a conference and has a car and motorbike to get around.

God is certainly blessing this man. He keeps on inviting me to come out again, but until the Lord heals my back that will not be possible.

The needs of the different ministries here in Northern India are great. They need help to function and win millions of the Hindu and Moslem people to the Lord. As I write this book, it is in the hope that some of you can become part of seeing Northern India won for the Lord, not only by your prayers but also by love-gifts.

It is not just a matter of evangelists going to India and sharing the Gospel, as they would in any other country. It is different here. Because of the high rate of illiteracy, these people have been brought up on oral stories. It is a well-known fact that their memories are far superior to ours who read literature.

People in India are unaccustomed to the Western-style of learning. They are more inclined to Biblical storytelling in cross-cultural contexts. There is a great need to people to become storytellers.

Paul Koehler, who was a missionary, has developed a program to train storytellers in their own languages and it has been a great success. Storytelling has been found to far superior for knowledge-transfer and for bypassing resistance to the gospel in oral contexts, thus presenting evidence of the effectiveness of biblical narrative among oral learners.

For interested readers, his book is called "Telling God's Stories with Power."

Chapter 27

The Way Ahead

Whilst completing this book, the Lord spoke with us to move to a town called San Miguel Escobar, which is a few miles away from where we live.

With all my back problems I thought it was time to call it a day, but no, the Lord spoke clearly to plant another church in this town. It concerned me a bit as the town was infamous for Mafia drug lords, but with the Lord's protection, we began a work there with the help of two new people in our life, Pastor Juan Carlos and his wife Miriam.

We prayed in our home for a few weeks until the Lord showed us a house in the town. Then the troubles began! I received a phone call from Miriam telling me they were at the local national hospital. Juan Carlos had great pain in his stomach and was vomiting. There were seventeen people before him in the line to be seen in the emergency room. One man actually died whilst waiting.

I drove to the hospital and told them to get into my car as I intended taking them to the local private hospital. Juan Carlos was operated on that day and was told had he arrived one hour later, he would be dead.

Later on, he was to die!

A week after the operation Juan Carlos went home, but a few days later he became very ill again. This time I took him to another local hospital where I knew the chief surgeon. He was operated on again twice! He stayed in the hospital for one month, but did not seem to be getting better. Each day I visited Juan Carlos, and along with Miriam, we prayed over him.

One morning, as I arrived at the hospital, a doctor friend of mine shook his head and walked by me. I knew at that moment Juan Carlos was dead. I rushed to his room. There were many people outside arguing amongst themselves, and Miriam would not let them in. They had tried for two hours to enter and I heard them talking about purchasing a coffin. People are buried here within twenty-four hours.

Miriam allowed me in… and there was Juan Carlos sitting up in bed! Miriam had refused to accept he was dead and prayed against the spirit of death. He had been dead two hours! God had given Miriam her wish.

This was now the second time I have experienced someone rising from the dead. What a God we serve!

It took Juan Carlos a month to recover, and the doctor advised he needed to rest. Our good missionary friends, Joe and Karin Bedford, allowed him to stay with them. They were not able to stay with us as we had dogs in our house and the doctor emphatically made it clear he should avoid dogs. We are very grateful to Joe and Karin Bedford for taking care of Juan Carlos and helping us raise the funds to pay a massive hospital bill. God took care of that and all the funds came in!

A few months later, we started our new church in earnest and soon we had a building not only for Juan Carlos and Miriam to live in, but also for the church services. Within a few weeks we had about fifty new converts in the church and it is still growing. We are now praying for the Lord to give us a much larger piece of land where we can construct a new church building and a house for Juan Carlos and Miriam.

This is the way forward and we believe for thousands of people to be saved in this new town. We want to see the drug lords won to Jesus, as well as many of the very poor people in this town. Jesus is Lord, and I have a fire in my bones to see healings and wonders. \

Please keep us in your prayers and ask your friends to read this book. I am praying that a fire will begin in their bones and that this fire will spread across Guatemala.

We want to see revival fires. We want to fill the stadiums with thousands of people crying out to God for His mercy and His love.

An after note: We now have our new church building right next door to the house: The church, "God of Love" is growing healthily!

Chapter 28

Are You Called to be a Missionary?

There are many pros and cons, but I want to assure you if God has spoken, He will make a way!

Firstly, you have to raise your own support, unless you're Southern Baptist, (in which case you get a free ride). This means some late nights, phone calls, emails, and basically a lot of time invested into building and maintaining a base of personal ministry supporters. Your standard of living will change dramatically. Or at least, you don't make as much as you could in the "real world," often doing the same thing.

Get used to not always receiving mail from your supporters. Remember they are praying for you each day and sending financial support. Be prepared to hear from some skeptics: "So, when are you going to get a *real* job?" This is frustrating and sometimes embarrassing, because the truth is that you really do *work*.

You might also get hassled for doing stuff that normal people don't even think twice about, like buying a new car, going shopping, or doing virtually anything that doesn't fit their idea of what a "missionary" looks like.

Yes, I've dealt with all of the above. However, most days, my "job" feels more like a dream – something I *get* to do, not *have* to do. **Being a missionary is worth it.** I gladly put it in long days and extra hours because this is something that I'm passionate about. I thank God for the opportunity to use my gifts and answer a call to do something meaningful. There really are a lot of advantages to doing work for the King.

Some of the advantages? Well, you get to travel. Enough said. You discover all kinds of interesting things about yourself and the country you are in. I think more than in other cases, you get to introspect when you work in missions. You are forced to depend on God every single day. Whether it's financial support or some other means of dependence, your faith tends to grow. You build new relationships and maintain them better because you need supporters. The bottom line is you stay in touch with people who are paying and sending your financial support. At first, this felt strange to me, but now I'm extremely grateful for it and it keeps me humble.

One piece of good advice never to forget – invest in people, not churches. Although some churches might support your work, remember pastors change and their vision changes as well. I have learned this advice probably too late in life. Invest in people!

You get invited to all kinds of events to speak. Whether it's church services, university classes, or some other event, you are often asked to share about the exotic nature of your work. If you do not get invited, then ask to visit the churches on a regular basis.

You get a "get into heaven free" card. Just kidding! Prayer is a part of work. Spending thirty minutes in prayer with a colleague can be considered a completely legitimate form of work. And you have the freedom to bring your faith into professional conversations.

Don't get any ideas that being a missionary is any less challenging or demanding than a regular 9-5 office job. Our job is tough and can be stressful, but it is also incredibly fulfilling and rewarding. At this point in my life, I can't think of anything better (other than marriage) to which I could be giving my time.

The *Globe Mission* organization who are situated in Germany, which we are part of, is one big family who is always there to help and give advice. In times of emergencies, they were the first ones to contact us and ask where they could help. The Directors are Andreas & Marion Pestke. They are German, but also speak English. They are always there to help you at any time.

I write to them every three months and share my thoughts, my pains, and my laughter. It does get lonely at times, but that is the price we are willing to pay to see people added to the Kingdom. If you really feel the call to missions, then I suggest you contact *Globe Mission* straight away. The telephone number and email is given at the back of this book.

Depending on what country you live in, you can contact the German, British, or USA Organization. You will never regret it!

Just recently they have a new outreach: "Globe Mexico."

Working for the King of kings takes our breath away. One day I want to hear the Lord Say, "Well done my good and faithful servant!"

Jeff G Mills

Globe Missionary

Fire in My Bones   Jeff Mills

About the Author

Jeff Mills is a "Globe Mission" missionary and evangelist. He is director of Final Harvest Ministries. Together with his wife Christa they have helped to plant three churches in Guatemala and have also seen thousands saved in India. Jeff, by the grace of God moves in healing and miracles and also moves in the prophetic word

Contact Us

If you would like to receive our monthly newsletter, please write to our email address below. We will gladly send you one and get to know you as well.

Our Address and Email.
Jeff & Christa Mills
Apartado 10
03901 Antigua
Guatemala
Central América
Email:
JeffGMills@Gmail.com
Christ.Mills@gmail.com
Website: www.finalharvestministries.net

German Mission Organization
Globe Mission e.V.
Gueterstrasse 37
46499 Hamminkeln
Tel: +49 (0) 2852 5086-0
Email: Office@globemission.org
Website: www.globemission.org

English Mission Organization
Globe UK
PO Box 29068
Dunfermiline
Fife KY11 4YJ
Scotland
Tel: +44 (0) 1383 731618
Email: Office@globe-uk.org
Website: www.globe-uk.org

USA Mission
Globe Missions International
PO Box 3040
Pensacola
FL 32516-3040

Printed in Great Britain
by Amazon